REAL FOOTY FANS QUIZ BOOK

COMPILED BY MART MATTHEWS

DEDICATION

This book is for Mick Lowrie, a Luton Town fan for well over 60 years. We washed directors' Jaguars together at a factory on freezing Saturday mornings to get the money to go to football somewhere in the afternoon, in the days when you could just decide which game you fancied at noon and walk in paying by cash. Happy days! In season 1963-64 we saw 44 matches together, including Blackburn's 8-2 Boxing Day win at Upton Park.

It is a damning indictment of the progress that is supposed to have taken place on our railways that 60 years later we could not have found a train on Boxing Day to get us to that game!

ACKNOWLEDGEMENTS

My thanks are due to Jules Gammond for giving me the opportunity to publish this book in the first place, and to Pat Morgan for his valuable editorial assistance in bringing the project to fruition.

Published by G2 Entertainment Ltd
© G2 Entertainment 2023

ISBN: 9781782815846

All rights reserved. No part of this publication may be reproduced, stored in a retrieval system, or transmitted in any form by any means, electronic, mechanical, photocopying, recording or otherwise, without the prior permission of the publishers.

Every effort has been made to ensure the accuracy of the information within this publication but the publishers cannot be held responsible for any errors or omissions. Views expressed are those of the author and do not necessarily represent those of the publishers.

PICTURE CREDITS: Action Images, Alamy

REAL FOOTY FANS' QUIZ BOOK

1. ANYTHING GOES PART 1
2. ANYTHING GOES PART 2
3. APPEARANCES
4. 'BOYS OF '66'
5. BRITISH CLUBS IN EUROPE PART 1
6. BRITISH CLUBS IN EUROPE PART 2
7. BROTHERS
8. CHAMPIONS LEAGUE 1993-2023 CLUBS
9. CHAMPIONS LEAGUE 1993-2023 PLAYERS
10. CRICKETING FOOTBALLERS
11. CRYPTIC CLUBS
12. CRYPTIC FA CUP FINAL GOALSCORERS
13. CRYPTIC MANAGERS
14. ENGLAND GOALKEEPERS
15. ENGLAND GOALSCORERS
16. ENGLAND MANAGERS
17. ENGLAND V GERMANY
18. ENGLAND IN THE WORLD CUP 1950-1982
19. ENGLAND IN THE WORLD CUP 1986-2022
20. EUROPA LEAGUE 2010-2023
21. EUROPEAN CUP 1956-1992 CLUBS
22. EUROPEAN CUP 1956-1992 PLAYERS
23. EUROPEAN CUP WINNERS' CUP 1961-1999
24. EUROS 1960-2020 – COUNTRIES
25. EUROS 1960-2020 – PLAYERS
26. FA CUP 1872-1939 – CLUBS
27. FA CUP 1872-1939 – PLAYERS
28. FA CUP 1946-1999 – CLUBS
29. FA CUP 1946-1999 – PLAYERS
30. FA CUP 2000-2022 – CLUBS
31. FA CUP 2000-2022 – PLAYERS
32. FA CUP CURIOSITIES PART 1
33. FA CUP CURIOSITIES PART 2
34. FA CUP GIANTKILLERS
35. FAIRS CUP 1958-1971
36. FATHERS AND SONS
37. FOOTBALL AROUND THE COUNTRY - LANCASHIRE
38. FOOTBALL AROUND THE COUNTRY - LONDON
39. FOOTBALL AROUND THE COUNTRY - THE MIDLANDS
40. FOOTBALL AROUND THE COUNTRY - THE NORTH EAST
41. FOOTBALL AROUND THE COUNTRY - SOUTH OF LONDON
42. FOOTBALL AROUND THE COUNTRY - YORKSHIRE
43. FOOTBALLER OF THE YEAR
44. FOOTBALL ODDITIES
45. GLOBETROTTING GOALIES
46. GOALSCORING GOALIES
47. GOALSCORING HEROES
48. GROUNDS (BUILT POST-SECOND WORLD WAR)
49. GROUNDS (GONE BUT NOT FORGOTTEN)

CONTENTS

50. GROUNDS IN GENERAL
51. HAT-TRICKS
52. INTERNATIONAL CAPS
53. KEEP ON KEEPING ON!
54. LEAGUE CUP 1960-1999 – CLUBS
55. LEAGUE CUP 1960-1999 – PLAYERS
56. LEAGUE CUP 2000-2022 – CLUBS
57. LEAGUE CUP 2000-2022 PLAYERS
58. LEAGUE TITLES 1888-1939
59. LEAGUE TITLES 1946-1992
60. PREMIER LEAGUE TITLES 1992-2022
61. LINKS
62. LOCAL DERBIES PART 1
63. LOCAL DERBIES PART 2
64. MANAGERS – BRITISH
65. MANAGERS – FOREIGN
66. NICKNAMES
67. OCCUPATIONS
68. ODD ONE OUT
69. ONE-CAP WONDERS PART 1
70. ONE-CAP WONDERS PART 2
71. ORIGINS
72. OUR NAME'S ON THE CUP
73. OWN GOALS
74. PENALTY! PART 1
75. PENALTY! PART 2
76. PLACES OF INTEREST
77. PLAY-OFFS 1987-2022
78. PREMIER PUZZLERS
79. PROMOTION AND RELEGATION PART 1
80. PROMOTION AND RELEGATION PART 2
81. QUOTES PART 1
82. QUOTES PART 2
83. REFEREES
84. SCOTLAND, WALES, NORTHERN IRELAND AND THE REPUBLIC OF IRELAND IN THE WORLD CUP
85. SCOTTISH FOOTBALL
86. SENT OFF PART 1
87. SENT OFF PART 2
88. SIX OF THE BEST!
89. SUPPORTERS' SONGS
90. TEN PLAYERS, PLEASE!
91. TRANSFER TRAIL
92. UEFA CUP 1972-2009
93. WHERE?
94. WORLD CUP 1930-1978 COUNTRIES
95. WORLD CUP 1930-1978 – PLAYERS
96. WORLD CUP 1982-2022 COUNTRIES
97. WORLD CUP 1982-2022 – PLAYERS
98. YOU'RE HIRED!
99. YOU'RE FIRED!
100. 'Z'

BONUS – THE QATAR WORLD CUP 2022

1 ANYTHING GOES PART 1

1. Which five drinks have been involved in the sponsorship of the English League Cup?

2. Which club won the English league title but failed to win away from home the following season?

3. To which country did England play away in the same city seven times before meeting them at home for the first time at White Hart Lane in 1933?

4. Alex Ferguson led Manchester United to 13 English league titles. Only one other post-World War Two manager with a surname beginning with 'F' has won the league. Who was he?

5. Which is the only country to have staged a World Cup final in two of its cities?

6. In the 1937-38 season which English club became not only the first to experience relegation the season after winning the league, but also the only side to go down despite scoring more goals than any other club?

7. Which country did England meet ten times without conceding a goal until a meeting at the Etihad Stadium in 2016?

8. Ian Porterfield became the first manager to be sacked in the English Premier League in 1993. Which club pulled the plug on him?

9. Who is the only player in the current century to be capped for England while at three 'Uniteds'?

10. Widely considered to be the greatest Italian club side after taking the first four post-war league titles, they were decimated in a plane crash when returning home from an away game in 1949. Who were they?

ANYTHING GOES PART 2

11. Which club has appeared in nine FA Cup semi-finals without ever winning the trophy?

12. Who are the only French club to win their league title in the 1950s, 1960s, 1970s and 1980s?

13. Alter one letter in the full name of a film star who appeared in The Dirty Dozen and you produce the name of a goalscorer in an FA Cup replay for Manchester United. Who is that player?

14. How are the international careers of Michael Owen, Emile Heskey, Phil Neville and Jamie Carragher connected?

15. Which is the smallest British city to have two of its teams reach a European Cup semi-final?

16. Over 2010-11 and 2011-12 Norwich City played 84 League games in two divisions. One of their goalkeepers played in 82 of them while another 'keeper appeared in the other two. If you take away the last letter of the main man's surname you are left with his understudy. Who are the two goalkeepers?

17. Two twins, David and Dean, were sacked as managers just three days apart in February 2013, at Lincoln City and Aldershot respectively. What surname did they share?

18. One of the greatest upsets in Scottish football took place at Parkhead on 8 February 2000 when Celtic were beaten 3-1 by Inverness Caledonian Thistle in the Scottish Cup third round. Who got the sack, who replaced him and what headline appeared in The Scottish Sun the next day?

19. Who played for Barcelona when they beat Real Madrid 5-0 in 1993-94 before, in the following season, playing for Real Madrid when they beat Barcelona 5-0?

20. What links Blackpool, Luton Town, Reading and Accrington Stanley?

3 APPEARANCES (CAN BE DECEPTIVE!)

21. Which goalkeeper between 1980 and 2003 made 773 English League appearances for nine clubs, three of which were on the south coast?

22. Which one of the 11 players that made up England's World Cup-winning side had the most league games to his name at the end of his career?

23. In a career that lasted from 1963 to 1984, which player turned out 743 times in the English League for just three London clubs and no others?

24. As well as being the only player to reach 1,000 league games, Peter Shilton has also been the only man to play more than 100 times for five clubs. Who are they?

25. David Seaman, Frank Worthington and Steve Bruce all played over 700 League games. Which club did all three play for?

26. Steve Perryman racked up 655 league outings for Spurs, and Ron Harris matched that figure exactly for Chelsea. Which other club did they both play for?

27. Which two post-Second World War goalkeepers with 1,548 League appearances between them both started out in English football at Watford?

28. You could say that this man was something of a rolling stone between 1968 and 1988, when he played 749 games for nine clubs. Who was he?

29. Between 1970 and 1989 goalkeeper Phil Parkes played a total of 688 times in League football for QPR and West Ham United. Which one did he play for the most?

30. Who, with 770, holds the record for the most English League games with one club, achieved between 1960 and 1980 at Swindon Town?

BOYS OF '66'   4

Banks, Cohen, Wilson, Stiles, J Charlton, Moore, Ball, Hunt, R Charlton, Hurst, Peters: England's iconic World Cup-winning team of 1966. But how much do you know about what happened to them afterwards?

31. Which two members of that team both went on to play for and manage Preston North End?

32. Which member of that team spent his entire career with one southern club?

33. Which member of that team ended his playing days at Bolton Wanderers?

34. Which member of that team was successful in just one other final in his career when Stoke City won the League Cup final in 1972?

35. Which member of that team went on to play for and manage Sheffield United?

36. Which member of that team scored a goal in a later FA Cup final?

37. Which member of that team managed Southend United in the 1980s?

38. Which member of that team went on to play for a team in red and white stripes before ending his career at a club that play in blue and white stripes?

39. Which member of that team went on to play in FA Cup finals for two different clubs before ending his career at Bristol Rovers?

40. Which member of that team finished up playing for Oldham Athletic and Bradford City?

5 BRITISH CLUBS IN EUROPE PART 1

I am excluding the European Super Cup, the Intercontinental Cup, the Club World Championship and the Club World Cup as I regard them as essentially meaningless.

41. Who are the only British club to play in two consecutive Cup Winners' Cup finals?

42. Who were the only British team to win the Fairs Cup twice?

43. Which two British clubs have won a European competition on Barcelona's ground, the first in a Cup Winners' Cup final and the second in a Champions League final?

44. Which city has been the location for wins in European finals by Aston Villa, Everton, Manchester United and Spurs?

45. Which three British clubs have won more European trophies than domestic league titles?

46. Which British club side, in 1960, became the first to appear in a European final when they lost in the Fairs Cup to Barcelona?

47. Which club has contested European finals against Arsenal, Spurs and West Ham United?

48. Which British club reached the semi-final of the very first European Cup of 1955-56?

49. Which club have met Aston Villa, Chelsea, Glasgow Rangers, Leeds United and Manchester United in European finals?

50. Which one of the following Welsh clubs has never reached the European Cup Winners' Cup quarter-final stage?
A. Cardiff City, B. Newport County C. Swansea City D. Wrexham

BRITISH CLUBS IN EUROPE PART 2   6

51. Which British club has both won and lost in a European final in Paris, against the same club each time?

52. Which ex-Manchester United striker broke Fulham hearts by scoring Atletico Madrid's winner in extra time in the 2010 Europa League final?

53. When Manchester United and Barcelona met each other in the European Cup Winners' Cup final of 1991, all the goals were scored by two men who later managed the same club. Who were the club and the two players?

54. Who was Chelsea's manager when they won the Europa League by beating Benfica in the 2013 final in Amsterdam?

55. Which British club is the only one to lose a UEFA Cup final with a 'silver goal'? It happened against FC Porto in 2003.

56. When Real Zaragoza beat Arsenal in the 1995 European Cup Winners' Cup final, the winning goal, a superb volley from the halfway line, brought more joy to Spurs fans than they would feel anyway at such a moment. Why?

57. Who were the only British club to lose in a UEFA Cup final in the 1980s when they were beaten by IFK Gothenburg in 1987?

58. Which British club lost two European finals in penalty shoot-outs 20 years apart?

59. Three players with countries for names have represented British clubs in a European final. They appeared for West Ham United, Spurs and Ipswich Town. Who were the three?

60. Liverpool's first experience of a European final came when they were beaten after extra-time by Borussia Dortmund in the 1966 European Cup Winners' Cup final. Where was the match played?

7 BROTHERS

61. A 5-1 win over Wales in 1966 at Wembley was the only occasion when which two brothers scored for England?

62. Which two brothers were part of the Chelsea side that lost to Spurs in the 1967 FA Cup final?

63. Which Brazilian twins have appeared for Manchester United in the Premier League this century?

64. Which two brothers won the FA Cup with Arsenal in 1950?

65. When Manchester United won the FA Cup against Liverpool in 1977, which two brothers helped them do it?

66. In the late 1980s three brothers lined up for Southampton against Sheffield Wednesday in a top-flight league fixture. Who were they?

67. Which two brothers, who won a fair few club trophies along the way at Old Trafford, also appeared 144 times between them for England?

68. Which two Chilean brothers were the toast of Tyneside when Newcastle United won the 1952 FA Cup final against Arsenal?

69. Which two Ivorian brothers have won the FA Cup this century, one with Arsenal and the other with Manchester City?

70. One brother played for Newcastle United in the 1974 FA Cup final while the other played and scored for Wolves in the same year's League Cup final. They also, while playing for those same clubs, scored against each other in a 1-1 draw. Who were they?

CHAMPIONS LEAGUE 1993-2023 – CLUBS

71. Apart from the two Champions League finals that concerned the two Madrid clubs, the only time that the names of the two finalists ended with the same letter came in the 2003-04 season. One beat the other 3-0. Who were they?

72. Who are the only club in this period to win the Champions League in two British cities, and which cities were the hosts?

73. Which two clubs – one from Italy and the other from Spain – are the only two to lose consecutive Champions League finals in this period?

74. Between 2006 and 2009, four English clubs lost in the Champions League final. Who were they?

75. The year 2012 saw the only occasion in this period when a team lost the Champions League on their own ground. Which club did this happen to?

76. When the ridiculous and highly misleading change of name for the competition took place in 1992-93, which French club won the first competition under the new heading?

77. Which Italian club appeared in the first three Champions League finals, winning one and losing two?

78. The 2013 final at Wembley produced the only occasion when two German clubs met each other in the final. Who were they?

79. Which club won the Champions League four times between 2006 and 2015?

80. Who are the only three clubs from the same city to appear in a Champions League final in this century?

9 CHAMPIONS LEAGUE 1993-2023 – PLAYERS

81. Who captained Manchester United to their Champions League final victory over Bayern Munich in 1999?

82. Which Englishman scored for Real Madrid when they won 3-0 in the 2000 final?

83. In the 3-3 draw between Liverpool and AC Milan in the 2005 final, who was the only player to score twice?

84. Who put Arsenal ahead when they lost 2-1 to Barcelona in the 2006 final in Paris?

85. AC Milan got their revenge on Liverpool for their penalty shoot-out win in 2005 by beating them 2-1 in Athens in the 2007 final. Who scored both Milan goals?

86. Who was sent off in extra time during the Manchester United v Chelsea final in Moscow in 2008?

87. Whose penalty in extra time of the Bayern Munich v Chelsea final of 2012 did Petr Čech save, eventually leading to the Londoners landing the trophy?

88. Who scored for Real Madrid in the last minute of the 2014 final against local rivals Atletico Madrid - a goal that produced extra time and a 4-1 win for Real?

89. Which Scottish international was a member of the Borussia Dortmund side that beat Juventus in the 1997 final?

90. Who is the only player over this 30-year period to win the Champions League with three clubs?

CRICKETING FOOTBALLERS   10

91. Which Australian goalkeeper who played for Bury, Bolton Wanderers and Stockport County between 1947 and 1957 played his cricket, unsurprisingly, with Lancashire at Old Trafford?
92. Between 1959 and 1975 he played over 500 times for Huddersfield Town, Carlisle United, Doncaster Rovers and Queen of the South while enjoying an excellent cricket career with Leicestershire and England. Who was he?
93. Arguably the most attractive batsman in the history of Middlesex, which Test cricketer was also seen dashing up the left wing for Arsenal?
94. West Ham's goalkeeper when they won the FA Cup for the first time in 1964 was also a bowler for Worcestershire, winning the county championship with them in the same year to complete an unusual double. Who was he?
95. Who scored for Manchester City in the 1956 FA Cup final against Birmingham City and also played cricket for Lancashire until 1964?
96. In the 1960s and 1970s, who played in goal for Aston Villa, Tranmere Rovers and WBA, and also represented Lancashire, Surrey, Worcestershire and Warwickshire in the summer game?
97. He played exactly 250 league games at right back for Huddersfield Town between 1953 and 1964 while also playing his part in the very successful Yorkshire team of that era, being capped for England along the way. Who was he?
98. This man shares his surname with a famous poet and played for Arsenal and Bristol City in the early 1950s. His cricketing career was notable for its longevity when he turned out for England and Gloucestershire between 1948 and 1974. Who was he?
99. Like the answer to the last question, he played for England at both sports. Leicestershire and Yorkshire were his cricketing affiliations, while with the larger ball he represented Huddersfield Town before the Second World War and Sunderland and Halifax Town after it. Who was he?
100. After six games up front for Bradford City in 1952, he became a great captain of Yorkshire, Somerset and England, exhibiting great courage and excellent tactical acumen. Who was he?

11 CRYPTIC CLUBS

Can you locate the equal mix of English and Scottish clubs from the clue given in each case?

101. What you have to do to keep a steam locomotive going.

102. Organs.

103. A practice often found in libraries.

104. Aged meat.

105. One half of legendary crime duo.

106. 6. Visited a lot in 1851.

107. Recent hit musical.

108. West Brom plus Blackburn.

109. Opposite of Preston.

110. Someone asks after a parent's health.

CRYPTIC FA CUP FINAL GOALSCORERS   12

You are given the year of the FA Cup final they scored in and a clue to their identity. Can you uncover the goalscorers?

111.   Football club – 1979

112.   Currency – 2019

113.   Found on letters – 1946

114.   Criminals – 1981 (came in a replay)

115.   Holiday destination in north Norfolk – 1999

116.   Sharing a surname and gathering dust – two players, 1956 and 1961

117.   Wartime shelter – 1948

118.   Elton John's cousin – 1959

119.   Sidekicks of two famous detectives and what those sleuths hope to solve – three players, 1950, 2013 and 1977

120.   Found in the Bible – three players, 1965, 1967 and 2019

13 CRYPTIC MANAGERS

121. Which prison has managed three London clubs in the current century?

122. Which item of clothing played in an FA Cup final for Watford before going on to manage them?

123. Which Premier League manager also had a hand in the Pink Panther theme?

124. He's a country, a river and a fashion model who has also found time to manage Bristol City, Stoke City and Hearts. Who is he?

125. Which Manchester United manager was also responsible for grave-digging, bell-ringing and other churchly duties?

126. It would have been appropriate if, instead of being the 21st man to be in charge of Spurs, he had been number 144! Who was he?

127. Which military headgear has accumulated five league titles?

128. Which two Sheffield United managers share their surnames with consecutive British prime ministers?

129. Which pop group has managed as far west as Yeovil, as far east as Grimsby, as far south as Brighton and as far north as Scarborough?

130. Which club have been managed by a South African city, a Derbyshire town, a Welsh town with an English railway station, a Merseyside town, a golfing legend and a razor blade?

ENGLAND GOALKEEPERS   14

131. If you add just one letter to the surname of a goalkeeper who played three times for England in the mid-1950s, you produce another England goalkeeper who gained 43 caps in the 1980s and 1990s. Who are the two men?

132. Similarly, if you add one letter in the middle of the surname of a goalkeeper who played eight times for England between 2007 and 2014, you obtain another goalkeeper who won six caps for England between 2014 and 2016. Who are the two goalkeepers?

133. Which two post-Second World War goalkeepers whose names begin with the same letter have both been capped while at Stoke City?

134. Who was unfortunate enough to be in England's goal when they lost 6-3 to Hungary at Wembley in 1953 and was still between the posts when they went down 7-1 in Budapest the following year?

135. Who are the only two goalkeepers to play for England while with five clubs?

136. In the 1950s a club who have never provided England with a goalkeeper before or since came up with two, namely Bernard Streten and Ron Baynham. Which club provided them?

137. Who played in goal in all five matches that England contested in the 2006 World Cup in Germany?

138. Which legendary Manchester City goalkeeper who played in goal for England in the late 1940s, after a career reduced by the war, lost his life in the Munich air crash in 1958?

139. Which goalkeeper from the current century has the unique record of playing four times for England while at four different clubs?

140. 10. Which two post-Second World War England goalkeepers both made 75 appearances in England internationals?

15 ENGLAND GOALSCORERS

141. England beat San Marino 6-0 and 7-1 in World Cup qualifiers in 1992 and 1993. One player got four goals in the first game and another got the same total in the second. Who were the two marksmen?

142. Prolific England goalscorers Tom Finney, Nat Lofthouse and Alan Shearer all scored the same number of goals for their country. How many?

143. Who is the only player to score a hat-trick for England while still in his teens?

144. Who was responsible for the first goal in the England managerial careers of both Glenn Hoddle and Sven-Göran Eriksson?

145. In the group stages of the 2004 Euros, which England player scored twice in a 3-0 win over Switzerland and then repeated the trick in a 4-2 victory against Croatia?

146. Which England international who made his debut for his country in 1980 is the only man to score inside 45 seconds in a Wembley international on two separate occasions?

147. When England went out of the 2010 World Cup, losing 4-1 to Germany, Frank Lampard scored a perfectly good goal that didn't count. Who scored the one that did?

148. Of all the players to score over 20 goals for England, Vivian Woodward (1903-11) and Steve Bloomer (1895-1907) have achieved something that none of the others have. What is it?

149. Who were the only two players to score for England in both the 1966 and 1970 World Cups?

150. Who is the only post-Second World War England international to score for his country in three different decades?

ENGLAND MANAGERS (AND CARETAKERS)   16

151. Which England manager lost as a player to Chelsea in an FA Cup final?

152. Which two England managers were on opposite sides when they led out their countries for the first match of the Euros at Wembley in 1996?

153. Who is the only England manager with a 100 per cent record?

154. Who is the only England manager to have played for Manchester United?

155. Which England manager lost his first game in charge of the national side 5-2 against France in Paris?

156. Which two England managers have also managed Wolves?

157. Which four England managers or caretaker managers had previously led a club to a League title in England?

158. Which England manager was appointed after Brazilian Luiz Felipe Scolari turned down the job?

159. Who are the only three England managers to have won league titles with clubs in more than one country?

160. Which four England managers or caretaker managers have also been in charge of Manchester City?

17 ENGLAND V GERMANY

161. In which five countries have England and Germany met in the final stages of World Cup tournaments?

162. In the final stages of the 2000 Euros the countries played each other in a Belgian town, with England coming out on top 1-0. Which town was it and who scored the vital goal?

163. You probably know about a particular game at Wembley in July 1966, but five months previously England and Germany contested a friendly on the same pitch with England winning 1-0. Which Manchester United man got the winner?

164. Which German forward played against England in the 1950s, 1960s and 1970s?

165. More amazing longevity, this time from the English side. Who appeared for winning teams against the Germans in 1935, 1938 and 1954?

166. Besides Wembley Stadium, only one other English ground has been used as the venue for an England v Germany encounter. England won the match 3-0 in 1935. On which London ground did it take place? A. Highbury B. Stamford Bridge C. Upton Park
D. White Hart Lane

167. When Germany beat England 4-1 in the 2010 World Cup, three members of their team later played for Arsenal in the Premier League. Who were they?

168. When England won 3-1 in Berlin in May 1956, three of their players were among those who lost their lives in the Munich air disaster two years later. Who were they?

169. In 1993 Germany beat England 2-1 in a friendly in which American city? A. Chicago   B. Detroit C. Los Angeles D. New York

170. In 2000 at Wembley a German playing his league football in England scored against England in a World Cup qualifier. One year later an Englishman playing his league football in Germany turned out for England in a World Cup qualifier in Munich. Who were the two players?

ENGLAND IN THE WORLD CUP 1950-1982   18

171. For which two World Cup tournaments did England fail to qualify in this period?

172. Who was the only player to represent England in their first three appearances in World Cups, in 1950, 1954 and 1958?

173. Which was the only country that England met in World Cups in the 1950s, the 1960s and the 1970s?

174. England have met the hosts in the opening game just once, beating them 2-0 in 1954. Who were they?

175. Everyone knows the England XI that got the job done in 1966. But which three members of that famous team didn't appear in all six matches?

176. England played five games in the 1982 World Cup in Spain. Who was their only player to find the net in more than one game?

177. You could have got good odds on this Wolves player being England's top scorer at the 1962 World Cup in Chile, but two goals from the penalty spot proved to be enough. Who was he?

178. Apart from Geoff Hurst's 1966 hat-trick in the final, only one other England player was on the mark twice in a World Cup match between 1958 and 1982. Who was he?

179. Which two Ipswich Town players appeared in all five of England's World Cup games in 1982?

180. When England were knocked out at the quarter-final stage by Brazil in 1962, their goal in the 3-1 defeat was, unusually for the time, scored by a player from a foreign club. Who was he and who did he play for?

21

19 ENGLAND IN THE WORLD CUP 1986-2022

181. Four players have scored from the penalty spot for England in World Cups in this period. Who are they?

182. In Mexico in 1986 England were in Group F alongside Morocco, Poland and Portugal. Who came out on top in that group?

183. In the 1990 World Cup tournament in Italy, Gary Lineker and David Platt scored seven of England's eight goals, if you count the one scored in the meaningless third-place game. Which defender scored the other one in a 1-0 win over Egypt?

184. Which three defenders chipped in with a goal apiece during England's journey to the semi-final in Russia in 2018?

185. Which country topped the group in which England finished bottom in Brazil in 2014?

186. Which African country did England beat in a thrilling quarter-final in 1990?

187. Which South American country did England win 3-0 against in the second round in 1986?
A. Bolivia B. Chile C. Paraguay D. Uruguay

188. Whose goalkeeping howler got England off to a bad start against the USA in the 2010 World Cup in South Africa, and which American player, who was plying his trade in the Premier League at the time, profited from it to score their goal in a 1-1 draw?

189. Only one Englishman scored in the first three World Cups of this century – in 2002, 2006 and 2010. Who was he?

190. In 1998 England faced a diverse trio in the group stage, coming up against countries whose names ended with the same two letters: one African, one South American and one European. Who were they?

EUROPA LEAGUE 2010-2023   20

191. Which British club were defeated in a penalty shoot-out in the Europa League final in 2021?

192. The only French club to reach the final of the Europa League did so in 2018, when they went down 3-0 to Atletico Madrid. Who were they?

193. Which club have been the only one to lose consecutive Europa League finals, in 2013 and 2014?

194. Spanish clubs have been very successful in the Europa League, in which Seville and Atletico Madrid have multiple wins to their names. Besides those two, who are the only Spanish side to win it, having done so in 2021?

195. Which manager who had previously taken charge of two Premier League clubs took Porto to victory in the Europa League when they beat Braga in the 2011 final in Dublin?

196. Who were the first Italian club to reach the Europa League final, going down 3-2 to Seville in 2020.

197. The first English club to contest a Europa League final were Fulham in the league's opening year of 2010, when they lost 2-1 to Atletico Madrid after extra time. Who scored their goal?

198. By hosting that first final in 2010 and another in 2020, which country became the first one to put on two finals on its soil?

199. Which two English teams contested the 2019 final, and in which city, against all reason, was the match held?

200. Manchester United's two Europa League finals have produced one win and one loss, and have yielded three goals. Their three goalscorers have all had spells in Italian football. Who are they?

21 EUROPEAN CUP 1956-1992 – CLUBS

201. In the 36 years that the competition was known as the European Cup, only one club with a colour in its name was successful. It happened after a penalty shoot-out in 1991. Who were they?

202. Real Madrid, dominating European football, won the first five finals from 1956 to 1960. Which team did they meet twice in the final between those years?

203. Nottingham Forest won the trophy in 1979 and 1980, in the middle of a great run for English clubs. The two cities in which they won began with the same letter. Which cities were they?

204. Which club won the European Cup for the first time at Wembley in 1992?

205. In the six years between 1971 and 1976 just two clubs won the European Cup, doing so three times each. Who were they?

206. Who, in 1984, became the only club in this period to lose a European Cup final on their own ground?

207. Who are the only two clubs to win the European Cup on their own ground, doing so in 1957 and 1965?

208. Who were the first club to win the European Cup in a penalty shoot-out?

209. On the only occasion that the final required a replay, Bayern Munich beat Atletico Madrid 4-0 after a 1-1 draw. In which year?

210. Celtic in 1967 and Manchester United in 1968 were the first two British clubs to lift the trophy. Which two clubs were beaten in those finals?

EUROPEAN CUP 1956-1992 – PLAYERS   22

211. Which Real Madrid player scored in all their five successful European Cup finals from 1956 to 1960?

212. Who was the first British player to hold the European Cup over his head?

213. Aston Villa's goalkeeper Jimmy Rimmer was injured in the warm-up for the 1982 final and had to be replaced after nine minutes. Who came on and kept a clean sheet as Villa won 1-0?

214. Whose penalty decided the final that should never have been played, between Juventus and Liverpool in 1986?

215. Who scored for Celtic in both their 1967 winning final and their losing one three years later?

216. When Real Madrid eventually lost a European Cup final in 1962, Benfica beat them 5-3. Which Real Madrid player scored a first-half hat-trick to no avail?

217. AC Milan's superb football exhibition against Steaua Bucharest saw them win the 1989 final 4-0. Which two Dutchmen each scored twice?

218. Who was the first man to score in both the 90 minutes and the extra-time period of a European Cup final?

219. Who was the only British player to score from the penalty spot in a European Cup final in this period?

220. When Feyenoord won the European Cup in 1970, one of their goals was scored by a player with a country for a name. Who was he?
A. Brazil B. Holland C. Israel D. Peru

23 EUROPEAN CUP WINNERS' CUP 1961-1999

221. Italian clubs bookended the competition in winning the first final in 1961 and the last one in 1999. Which two clubs were involved?

222. Which European city hosted six European Cup Winners' Cup finals?
A. Berlin B. London C. Rotterdam D. Vienna

223. British clubs enjoyed this competition, with nine of them winning it. How many can you name, and which one of the nine won it twice?

224. In the 1963 final between Spurs and Atletico Madrid a particular surname appeared on the team sheets of both clubs. What was it?
A. Brown B. Jones C. Smith D. White

225. An Englishman has the honour of being the only player to score in a final and the subsequent replay. Who is he?

226. Which club between 1976 and 1978 became the only one to play in three successive finals?

227. Which player with Chelsea connections scored twice in extra time in 1990 against Anderlecht to take the trophy to Sampdoria?

228. In this whole period only one final was decided by a penalty. It came in Barcelona's 1-0 win over Paris St-Germain in 1997. Who scored it?

229. Four British winners of the ECWC have fielded a player with the same surname. What is that surname and who are the four clubs?

230. What did Rob Rensenbrink do in the late 1970s that nobody else has done before or since in the competition?

EUROS 1960-2020 COUNTRIES   24

231. In the 2016 final France lost to a country they had beaten in their ten previous meetings. Who were they?

232. Which country, in 2012, became the first to retain the trophy?

233. Between 1972 and 1980 which country appeared in three successive finals?

234. They won the first competition in 1960, but were subsequently beaten in the finals of 1964, 1972 and 1988. Who were they?

235. Which country, which was defeated in two of the first three finals, now no longer exists?

236. One of the lowest points in England's footballing history came in the 1988 Euros, when they lost all three group matches. Which three countries combined to send them home early?

237. Who are the only country to both win and lose a Euro final on their own soil?

238. In 2004 the two countries that played each other in the very first game were also the two countries that contested the final. Who were they?

239. Which two countries that begin with the same letter knocked England out of the tournament in 2016 and 2020?

240. A war allowed a country that hadn't qualified for the 1992 Euros the chance to take part. They took the opportunity with both hands by winning the thing! Who were they, and why was it even more special than it sounds?

25 EUROS 1960-2020 PLAYERS

241. Who was the only player to score in three of England's four matches in the 2004 tournament?

242. Who scored the winning goal when Spain defeated Germany in the 2008 final?

243. Only one man found the net in all three group matches in the 2016 competition. Who was he?

244. In their opening group game of 2004, England led France going into the 90th minute yet somehow contrived to concede not once, but twice in the remaining moments. Which Frenchman was the beneficiary of England's lapses with the two goals that turned the game?

245. Which player who spent some time in English football scored from the penalty spot for the Czech Republic when they lost 2-1 to Germany in the Wembley final of 1996?

246. Which future Fulham manager played in the French side that won the trophy in 1984?

247. Who is the only Englishman to score in the final?

248. Who was the scorer of the 'golden goal' whereby France prevailed against Italy in the 2000 final in Rotterdam?

249. The 2012 final between Spain and Italy was the first time that the captains in the Euros final were the two goalkeepers. Who were they?

250. Three Germans have scored twice in Euros finals. They were Horst Hrubesch in 1980, Oliver Bierhoff in 1996 and which player in 1972?

FA CUP 1872-1939 CLUBS   26

251. Which team won the FA Cup five times in the first seven years of its existence?

252. Which two clubs who were not that far apart geographically were the first to play each other three times in the FA Cup final when they met in the finals of 1887, 1892 and 1895?

253. Who are the only club still playing League football to win the FA Cup three years in a row?

254. In the 1922 final a Yorkshire club beat a team from Lancashire 1-0 in the FA Cup final. However, the situation was reversed in 1938 when the Lancastrians beat that same Yorkshire side by the same score. Who were the two teams?

255. The team with the shortest name of any FA Cup winners also have a record in finals that others might envy. Their only two finals, in 1900 and 1903, brought wins of 4-0 and 6-0. Who were they?

256. In 1912, who became the only Yorkshire club to win the FA Cup on Yorkshire soil when they beat WBA in a replay at Bramall Lane?

257. Who were the only two 'Cities' to win the FA Cup before the First World War?

258. Which team who never played League football are the only one to play in six FA Cup semi-finals and win them all?
A. Old Carthusians B. Old Etonians C. Oxford University
D. Royal Engineers

259. The only time the FA Cup left England came with the victory of Cardiff City in 1927. Which side, appearing in their first final, did they beat 1-0 to land the prize?

260. Which Lancastrians took the trophy home with them three times in the 1920s? A. Blackburn Rovers B. Blackpool C. Bolton Wanderers
D. Burnley

27 FA CUP 1872-1939 PLAYERS

261. The only goalkeeper with a three-letter surname to play in an FA Cup final in the first 100 years of the competition gained a winner's medal on the three occasions he did so: in 1923, 1926 and 1929. Who was he?

262. Who, in 1923, scored the first ever goal in an FA Cup final at Wembley and, in 1930, played for Arsenal in the FA Cup final after joining them for a record fee?

263. Which legendary Derby County player whose statue adorns their current ground scored for them in their losing 1898 final against rivals Nottingham Forest?

264. What was unique about Fred Keenor's FA Cup experience in 1927?

265. The three goals that won the FA Cup final replay for Spurs against Sheffield United in 1901 were scored by three players who share their surnames with post-Second World War leaders of British political parties: two Labour and one Conservative. Who were the three goalscorers?

266. One of Newcastle United's goalscorers in their 1924 FA Cup final win over Aston Villa later went on to manage the Geordies to further success in the competition. Who was he?

267. He played for England at football and cricket, equalled the world long jump record, dabbled in politics and academia and still found time to play for Southampton in the 1902 FA Cup final against Sheffield United. Who was he?

268. Unusually, all the scorers' surnames in the 1908 final began with the same letter. They were Hunt, Hedley, Harrison and Howie. Which two clubs, who have now won the trophy ten times between them, contested that final?

269. In appearing for Manchester United in 1909, Aston Villa in 1913 and Chelsea in 1915, who became the first man to play in an FA Cup final for three different clubs?

270. Who became the only player to score twice in a 1920s FA Cup final when he helped Blackburn Rovers beat Huddersfield Town in 1928?

FA CUP 1946-1999 CLUBS 28

271. Which club lost the four FA Cup finals they contested between 1949 and 1969?

272. Which three clubs in this period were the only ones to play in three successive FA Cup finals?

273. Which club were defeated in the 1948 and 1951 finals before their highly emotional victory in 1953?

274. In successive years in the 1980s two clubs appeared in their first FA Cup finals and ended up winning the trophy. Who were they?

275. Who were the first London club to win the FA Cup in this period?

276. Who are the only club to be involved in an FA Cup final in all six decades of this section?

277. Which two clubs did Arsenal meet more than once in FA Cup finals over this period?

278. Which two clubs played in an FA Cup final for the first time in the 1970s?

279. Who were the most southerly club to win the FA Cup during this period?

280. The following three FA Cup finals all went to extra time, but they were not alone in that. What, however, does differentiate them from the other 51 finals of this period?
Derby County v Charlton Athletic – 1946
Liverpool v Leeds United – 1965
Chelsea v Leeds United – 1970

29 FA CUP 1946-1999 PLAYERS

281. Who was the only man to win the FA Cup as a player-manager in this period?

282. In the last two decades of the 20th century, who played in five FA Cup finals for three clubs?

283. Who was the only player to score twice from the penalty spot in an FA Cup final in this period?

284. Who appeared in three FA Cup finals for Everton in the 1980s and another for Sunderland in the 1990s but failed to get his hands on a winner's medal?

285. He played as an amateur inside forward for Blackpool in the 1951 FA Cup final and captained Wolves as a centre half in 1960 when they won the trophy. He died in 2018 at the age of 91. Who was he?

286. As a manager he won the League, the FA Cup and a trophy in Europe, but in the 1964 FA Cup final, many years before all that, he became, at 17, the youngest ever player in an FA Cup final when he turned out for Preston North End against West Ham United. Who was he?

287. Which man in the 1960s appeared in an FA Cup final for both Manchester United and Leeds United?

288. They called the 1953 event 'The Matthews Final'. But he didn't score a hat-trick in that game. Who did score what turned out to be the only one in this period?

289. Who played for one London club in the 1964 final and another London club in the 1975 final?

290. The only palindromic goalscorer in an FA Cup final in this period scored for Newcastle United against Manchester City in the 1955 final. Who was he?

FA CUP 2000-2022 CLUBS   30

291. Which club was successful in both the last final at the 'old' Wembley in 2000 and the 'new' Wembley in 2007?

292. Who were the only club in this period to have the bittersweet experience of winning the FA Cup and being relegated in the same season?

293. Who were the only club between 2000 and 2022 to win consecutive FA Cup finals on two separate occasions?

294. The FA Cup final was played at the Millennium Stadium between 2001 and 2006. The same team won the first and last finals there. Who were they?

295. Who were the only Midlands side to appear in more than one FA Cup final in this period?

296. Four clubs made their FA Cup final debuts between 2000 and 2022. Which one of the four was the only one who had previously won the League Cup?

297. Which side were the only one in this period to score three goals in an FA Cup final and not take home the trophy?

298. Which club, defeated in a semi-final replay in 1930, finally got to the final in 2014, only to lose to the same club that had halted their progress to the final 84 years before?

299. Which three clubs who collectively have won the FA Cup 20 times failed to make an appearance in any final during this period?

300. Which two clubs met each other in three FA Cup finals between 2002 and 2020?

31 FA CUP 2000-2022 PLAYERS

301. When Millwall reached the FA Cup final in 2004, one of their players had already appeared in finals for two other clubs, while another would go on to play for another club in the final of 2009.
Who were the two players?

302. Who was the only player to score in four FA Cup finals during this period?

303. Besides the answer to the previous question, which other player has found the net in successive FA Cup finals during this period?

304. In 2009 who scored the fastest goal in an FA Cup final at Wembley, timed at 25 seconds?

305. Who are the only two players between 2000 and 2022 to score twice each in the same FA Cup final?

306. The Chelsea v Portsmouth final of 2010 saw two penalties awarded, one for each side. They failed to produce a single goal. Which two players missed them?

307. Which player missed from the spot in the penalty shoot-out to decide the outcome of the 2005 FA Cup final?

308. Who became the first goalkeeping substitute to get on to the pitch in an FA Cup final when Southampton's Antti Niemi was injured two thirds of the way through their 2003 final against Arsenal?

309. A Dutchman, a Belgian and a Frenchman are the only three men to score from the penalty spot in an FA Cup final between 2000 and 2022. Who are they?

310. Which player ended up on the losing side in both his appearances in an FA Cup final, first with West Ham United in 2006 and then with Stoke City five years later?

FA CUP CURIOSITIES PART 1   32

311. Why were Darlington knocked out of the FA Cup twice in the 1999-2000 season, first by Gillingham and then by Aston Villa?

312. In the 1984 final between Everton and Watford there was a former British prime minister on both sides. Who were they?

313. Which two players in QPR's forward line in the 1982 final against Spurs together produce a singing duo from long ago who were also members of the 'Crazy Gang'?

314. If you put Arsenal's opening goalscorer in their 1930 FA Cup final against Huddersfield Town in front of one of Everton's goalscorers in their 1933 final against Manchester City, you produce a legendary 1950s American actor. Who?

315. Which surname could be found in Newcastle United's FA Cup final teams of 1955 and 1998?

316. Which two fruits, one for Leeds United and the other for Southampton, appeared in FA Cup finals in the 1970s?

317. Between 1973 and 1978 three FA Cup finals produced a detective who lived in Baker Street, his trusty right-hand man and his landlady! Who were the three players and their clubs?

318. Roger played in the 1957 FA Cup final, Johnny in 1964, Gerry in 1965 and John in 1992. What surname do they share and which clubs did they play for?

319. Which surname could be found in the FA Cup finals of 1978, 1979, 1980, 1982 and 1984?

320. The scorer of Birmingham's goal when they lost to WBA in the 1931 final was a football club and a city. Who was he?

33 FA CUP CURIOSITIES PART 2

321. Birmingham City's full backs in the 1956 FA Cup final against Manchester City together produce an appropriate greyhound stadium that closed in 2017 after 90 years. Who were those full backs?

322. Which fish who appeared in Dad's Army won the FA Cup with West Ham United in 1980?

323. Many players have said they are 'over the moon' after scoring, but who went one better than that after scoring for Arsenal against Newcastle United in the 1998 FA Cup final?

324. A member of Manchester United's FA Cup-winning team of 1948 and a member of the Spurs side that won the same trophy in 1981 together produce a well-known football club. Which one?

325. A maritime hero lost and won an FA Cup final with Cardiff City in 1925 and 1927 before returning to Wembley to win it again with Newcastle United in 1932. Who was he?

326. Which European football club played for Manchester United in the FA Cup finals of 2016 and 2018?

327. Which member of England's World Cup-winning side of 1966 joined three clubs who had the FA Cup in their boardrooms when he arrived but never won it himself?

328. Which non-League club opened the scoring in the 2014 FA Cup final?

329. Which three goalkeepers have captained their teams to victory in an FA Cup final in the last 35 years?

330. Which is the only city besides London that has staged an FA Cup final on more than one ground?

FA CUP GIANTKILLERS 34

331. Who was in charge of the the Third Division side Bournemouth when they beat the FA Cup holders Manchester United 2-0 in the third round in 1984 at Dean Court?

332. Which top-flight club lost at home to non-League Altrincham in the FA Cup in 1986, and on the same ground to Kidderminster Harriers, another non-League outfit, eight years later when in the second tier?

333. Their great run of giantkilling began with a 2-1 win over Sunderland in 1949 and subsequent years have made them famous for pulling off Cup shocks. Who are they?

334. A low point in Liverpool's history came when they were knocked out of the FA Cup in the third round in 1959 by a non-League side. The upside was that it ended up with the arrival on the scene of Bill Shankly. Who beat them?

335. The football result nobody could believe came in the third round in 1933 when Arsenal, the era's dominant club, were humbled 2-0 by which Midlands side?

336. Leeds United's much-feared side went out in the fifth round of the FA Cup in 1971 to a team from the fourth level of English football. Who were they?

337. Fresh from their League Cup exploits of two years before, Bradford City were at it again in 2015 in the FA Cup when the side from the third level disposed of two Premier League clubs in the fourth and fifth rounds. Who were they?

338. Which four non-League sides had shocks in store for Newcastle Utd in 1972, Burnley in 1975, Coventry City in 1989 and Leeds Utd in 2009?

339. I was one of the 16,000 squeezed into Aldershot's tiny Recreation Ground on a magical night in January 1964. A Dave Jones penalty save the previous Saturday had brought a First Division team south for the replay. At the time, they had won the FA Cup more times than any other club, but Aldershot beat them 2-1. What a night! Who were knocked out?

340. In 2013 a non-League club won away in the FA Cup to a Premier League side. Fifty-four years before they had met in the semi-final when the non-League side had been in the top flight and the Premier League side had been in the third tier. Who were the two clubs?

35 FAIRS CUP 1958-1971

341. Which Spanish club won the first two Fairs Cup finals in 1958 and 1959? A. Atletico Madrid B. Barcelona C. Real Madrid D. Real Zaragoza

342. Who are the only English club to win the Fairs Cup twice?

343. Which English club reached two successive Fairs Cup finals, in 1960 and 1961, but lost them both?

344. Which English team overcame a 3-1 deficit from the first leg to win the 1970 Fairs Cup 4-3 on aggregate?

345. The only Italian club to win the Fairs Cup did so in 1961. Who were they? A. AC Milan B. Fiorentina C. Juventus D. Roma

346. Which English club's only trophy in the last half-century came when they won the Fairs Cup in 1969?

347. Which Spanish club won the Fairs Cup two years running in 1962 and 1963? A. Athletic Bilbao B. Barcelona C. Real Madrid D. Valencia

348. Which Hungarian club won the trophy in 1965 and reached the final again in 1968?

349. In the first year of the competition England was represented by a team made up from London clubs. After a 2-2 draw in the first leg they were slaughtered 6-0 away in the second leg.
On which London ground did that first leg take place?
A. Highbury B. Stamford Bridge C. Wembley D. White Hart Lane

350. Two Englishmen who together scored 580 League goals in their careers were responsible for the first and last goals in a Fairs Cup final by English players, the first coming for the London team of 1958 and the last for Leeds United in 1971. Who were the two goalscorers?

FATHERS AND SONS   36

351. Which father and son have both won the Premier League as goalkeepers?

352. The father represented Manchester United in three 1990s FA Cup finals, while his son appeared in the 2014 final with Hull City. Who are they?

353. The father gained two England caps, but the son, in this century, reached three figures after making his England debut when at the same club his father was at when he won his two. Who were they?

354. The father won the FA Cup with Manchester United in 1948 and the son won the European Cup with the same club on the same ground 20 years later. Who were they?

355. Between them they won 16 England caps and the son was playing for the club his father was managing when he appeared for England for the first time in 1989. Who were they?

356. Between them they won 69 England caps. The father played in 1990s FA Cup finals for clubs from north and south London, while the son's career took in two clubs from the west side of the capital. Who were they?

357. The son played under his father at Southampton in the early years of this century. Who are they?

358. On 4 April 1996 history was made when Arnór Gudjohnsen was subbed for his son Eidur after 62 minutes in a 3-0 international win over Estonia. Which country were they playing for?

359. The father, Alan, kept goal for Preston North End in the 1964 FA Cup final, and then in 1990 two of his sons, Alan Junior and Gary, played in goal against each other in a third-tier game between Bury and Preston North End. What was the family name?

360. They once, in 1951, played in the same Stockport County side, but father Alec won the FA Cup with the blue half of Manchester in 1934 while son David won it with the red half in 1963. What surname is involved?

37 FOOTBALL AROUND THE COUNTRY: LANCASHIRE

361. Who were the first Lancastrian club to play in a League Cup final?

362. Who were the only team from Lancashire to lose an FA Cup final in both the 1950s and 1960s?

363. Which two Lancastrian towns are the only two to meet each other in an FA Cup final? It proved to be a memorable occasion.

364. Which Lancastrians restored their League status by winning the Vanarama National League in the 2021-22 season?

365. Who were the last town club from Lancashire to lift the FA Cup?

366. The fact that the first FA Cup final to be attended by a reigning monarch happened to be the 1914 renewal might have had something to do with war recruitment. Which Lancashire town club beat Liverpool 1-0 in the final?

367. Which Lancastrian city club had already won the League Cup twice before any other team in the region had won it at all?

368. Two Lancastrian town clubs contested League Cup finals in the 1990s, losing to Nottingham Forest and Liverpool in 1990 and 1995. Who were the two clubs?

369. After Blackburn Olympic and Blackburn Rovers' 19th century exploits in the competition, who became the next Lancashire town club to land the FA Cup when they were successful in 1900?

370. In a taste of the forthcoming excitement generated by the arrival of the Football League in 1888, two Lancastrian town clubs drew 5-5 with each other in their first game. One of them has three League titles to their name while the other has drawn a blank. Who were the two clubs?

FOOTBALL AROUND THE COUNTRY: LONDON   38

371. Which London club is the only one to have won all its home league games in a season? They produced this remarkable feat in Division Three South over 21 matches in 1929-30.

372. Who were the last London club to win the FA Cup before the Second World War?

373. Who were the first London club to win a European trophy on London soil?

374. A London club became, in the 1936-37 season, the first League side from outside the top two divisions to reach an FA Cup semi-final. Who were they?

375. Outside of the big three of Arsenal, Chelsea and Spurs, who were the last London club to finish runners-up in the League?

376. On Boxing Day 1963 there were 66 goals in ten First Division games. Which London club led the way with a 10-1 home win over Ipswich Town?

377. In 1959 Vic Rouse became the first player to be capped while playing in the fourth tier of English football when he was selected in goal for Wales. Which London club, for which he appeared in 238 League games, was he with at the time?

378. Leaving aside the 'big three' again, who were the last London team to win the FA Cup?

379. They came into the top flight after achieving promotion alongside Liverpool in 1961-62, but whereas the Merseysiders have done rather well since, this club were relegated in their first season up with the big boys and have never returned. Who are they?

380. One London club has won the FA Cup on another London club's ground. Can you name the Cup winners and the ground?

39 FOOTBALL AROUND THE COUNTRY: THE MIDLANDS

For our purposes 'the Midlands' comprises Aston Villa, Birmingham City, Coventry City, Derby County, Leicester City, Nottingham Forest, Notts County, Stoke City, Walsall, West Brom and Wolves.

381. Which two clubs from the same city both won the FA Cup in the 1890s?

382. Two famous goalkeepers, Bert Williams and Phil Parkes, both began their careers at which Midlands club?

383. Which Midlands club in 1931 completed a unique double by winning the FA Cup and promotion to the top flight in the same season?

384. February 1979 saw the first million-pound domestic transfer when one Midlands club sold its star player to another Midlands club. Which player was sold and which two clubs were involved in the transaction?

385. Before Leicester City's 2021 success in the competition, who were the last Midlands club to win the FA Cup and in what year?

386. Which Midlands club won the first post-war FA Cup final of 1946?

387. Who were the only two Midlands clubs to win the League title in the 1970s and which manager provides a link between them?

388. Which Midlands club won the FA Cup in the last year before the 1950s and the first year after it, drawing a blank in between despite it being by far the greatest decade in their history?

389. Which two Midlands clubs met in the 1964 League Cup final?

390. Which five of the 11 clubs listed at the top of the page have never won the League title?

FOOTBALL AROUND THE COUNTRY: NORTH EAST 40

391. Who is the only man in the post-Second World War era to win the FA Cup with one North East club as a player and then return to Wembley to repeat the trick as a manager with a different club from that area?

392. It was as long ago as 1936 when the League title last found itself this far north. Which club won it?

393. Who is the only man to captain Middlesbrough, Newcastle United and Sunderland?

394. Middlesbrough and Newcastle United have both appeared in European finals with contrasting experiences, Newcastle winning theirs in the 1960s and Middlesbrough losing out in 2006. Which two clubs provided the opposition?

395. With which three clubs from the North East was Brian Clough associated as a player or manager?

396. The North East has a strong non-League tradition and this was upheld at Wembley when which team won the FA Vase three years running between 2009 and 2011?

397. Going further back, amateur football was dominated by two teams from the area after the Second World War. Between them they won seven FA Amateur Cup finals at Wembley from the mid-1950s to the mid-1960s. Who were they?

398. The Feethams was the venue for an exciting local derby that ended in a 5-5 draw on 21 November 1936. Which two teams took part?

399. After accounting for top-flight Liverpool in the third round, which club from the North East reached the FA Cup quarter-final in 1952-53 while playing in the Third Division North, finally going down 1-0 at home to eventual finalists Bolton Wanderers?

400. In the post-war era six managers of the England national team have also been in charge of Middlesbrough or Newcastle United. Who are the six?

41 AROUND THE COUNTRY SOUTH OF LONDON

401. Which non-League club from the South West held Manchester United to a 0-0 draw at Old Trafford in the FA Cup third round of season 2004-05?

402. Which other club besides Gillingham has played its home games at Priestfield Stadium in the not too distant past?

403. Which club registered its record League victory when winning 8-0 against Birmingham City at St Andrew's in the 2014-15 season?

404. Only one club south of London has won the League title. Which one?

405. Brighton & Hove Albion have had two post-Second World War managers with identical names. One held the post from 1974 to 1976, while the other was there from 2001 to 2002.
What name do they share?

406. On 9 March 1901, England beat Ireland 3-0 in the first international to be played on a ground south of London. What was the venue?

407. Which club from the South West experienced the best FA Cup run in their history when they reached the semi-final in 1984, only to lose narrowly to Watford?

408. What have Jack Tinn and Harry Redknapp done that nobody else has?

409. Which club from the South West lost in the play-offs in 1988 but escaped from the Fourth Division by the same process against Blackpool on penalties in 1991?

410. Southampton were the first club from south of London to reach the FA Cup final when they appeared in 1900 and 1902. They lost both affairs, going down in the first one to a Lancastrian side and in the latter to one from Yorkshire after a replay. Which two clubs beat them?

AROUND THE COUNTRY 42
YORKSHIRE

411. Which four Yorkshire clubs have played in a League Cup final?

412. Between 1957 and the early years of this century, which five goalkeepers represented England while with a Yorkshire club?

413. Which Yorkshire club set a new record for away League wins in a season in 1946-47 when they were successful in 18 of their 21 games on the road, in the process taking the Third Division North title?

414. Who are the only Yorkshire club to win the League three times in a row; the only one to be runners-up three times in a row; and the only one to finish third three times in a row?

415. Who were the last two Yorkshire clubs to meet each other in an FA Cup semi-final and what was the score?

416. The only time that the FA Cup stayed in the county for two years was when Yorkshire clubs won it in 1911 and 1912. Which two sides did Yorkshire proud?

417. Which Yorkshire club set a new record of 43 League One matches unbeaten from New Year's Day of 2011 to November 28 of the same year?

418. Between 1965 and 1979 two forwards were capped for England while at both Sheffield United and Leeds United and no other clubs. Who were they?

419. Which Yorkshire team that sadly left the Football League in 1970 had previously, in 1926-27 and 1927-28, set a new record for successive home wins with 25 in Division Three North?

420. The nearest this Yorkshire club had got to Wembley was in reaching the FA Cup semi-final in 1955, but then, in the next century, they won twice there in the space of nine days to take the FA Trophy final and return to the Football League via the Conference play-off final. Who were they?

45

43 FOOTBALLER OF THE YEAR

There are two 'Footballer of the Year' awards. The first, starting in 1948, was the Football Writers' Association award, while the second, from 1974, was the Professional Footballers' Association award. In these questions I will call them the FWA and the PFA.

421. Who, in 1993, became the only Sheffield Wednesday player to win either award when he took the FWA trophy?

422. Who became the only man to win the award with a relegated club when he won the FWA variety with West Ham United in 2011?

423. Between 1965 and 1974, which four Leeds United players won either award?

424. During Leicester City's amazing 2015-16 season they scooped both awards. Which two players were involved, although personally I would have chosen another Leicester player?

425. That player finally got his hands on both awards the following season in the same coloured shirt but with another club. Who was he?

426. Which four foreign players won the FWA award while with Arsenal between 1998 and 2012?

427. Between 1956 and 1985 five goalkeepers became Footballer of the Year. Can you name them?

428. Which four players have won an award with two clubs?

429. In the first three years of this century the PFA version was won by three Manchester United players. Who were they?

430. Aston Villa have had no luck with the FWA award but their players have been successful three times in the PFA version: in 1977, 1990 and 1993. Which three men won it?

FOOTBALL ODDITIES　　　44

431. What unusual fact linked the 16 fourth round FA Cup ties of 1956-57 to those of season 2007-08?

432. In the late 1990s Fulham had a midfielder whose full name was the exact reverse of another midfielder who played for the club in the early 2000s. Who were the two men?

433. Which team that lost the 1971 European Cup final at Wembley to Ajax had 11 players whose names all ended with the same letter, which was also the last letter of the team's name?

434. In season 1928-29, Cardiff City finished bottom of the First Division and were relegated. What was extremely unusual about it?

435. Two of England's players in the 1970 World Cup tournament in Mexico together had surnames that refer to a hit-making singing duo of the time. Who were they?

436. The complete name of an Arsenal full back of the 1960s, 70s and 80s is the first name of a Manchester United full back of the 21st century. Who are the two men?

437. Which First Division club beat Burnley 8-3 on 24 October 1925 and then lost 8-3 to Sheffield United just two days later?

438. The first man is a winger who played 79 times for England between 1983 and 1996. The second man is a full back who played 36 times for England between 2002 and 2010. Together, they produce a south-west London railway station. Which one is it?

439. Which ground had 42 League games played on it in the 1946-47 season?

440. Which two players with the same surname have each scored for six different Premier League clubs this century?

45 GLOBETROTTING GOALIES

441. Which Dutch goalkeeper was sent off along with Everton's Francis Jeffers while playing for Liverpool in an Anfield Merseyside derby in September 1999?

442. Which goalkeeper whose name sounds like his nationality won the FA Cup four times with one club in this century, before ending his career as an unused substitute in a winning final for another club?

443. Which three Americans have guarded Tottenham Hotspur's net in the Premier League?

444. He was the recipient of an FA Cup winner's medal in 2017, and the following year faced England in the World Cup. Who is he, which club did he play for and which country did he represent?

445. In the 1990s, Norwegian goalkeepers appeared in FA Cup finals for Spurs and Chelsea. Who were they?

446. Who became the first Argentinian goalkeeper to win the League Cup when he performed heroics for Manchester City against Liverpool in the penalty shoot-out to decide the 2016 final?

447. Which two German goalkeepers whose names start with the same letter have played for Arsenal in the Premier League era?

448. West Ham's Czech goalkeeper had an amazing game against Manchester United at Upton Park on the last day of the 1994-95 season when he almost single-handedly stopped the visitors overhauling Blackburn Rovers in the title race. The welcome he received at Ewood Park the following season was long and loud. Who was he?

449. A Spanish goalkeeper turned out in three FA Cup finals for Liverpool in this century, and then neighbours Everton signed another FA Cup-winning Spanish 'keeper whose name began with the same letter as the earlier one. Who were the two Spaniards?

450. In the consecutive FA Cup finals of 2007, 2008 and 2009 the losing goalkeepers were a Dutchman, a Finn and an American. Who were the three?

GOALSCORING GOALIES 46

451. Which England international goalkeeper scored for two clubs in the first decade of this century, once in the Premier League against Watford and also in the League Cup against Swindon Town?

452. During the Premier League fixture between Stoke City and Southampton on 2 November 2013, one 'keeper scored past the other. Their first names and surnames matched each other. Who were they?

453. An on-loan goalkeeper kept Carlisle United in the League on 8 May 1999 by netting the winner in the last seconds of their home game with Plymouth Argyle and sending Scarborough into the Conference instead of the Cumbrians. Who was he?

454. Which goalkeeper scored with a header for Sheffield Wednesday against Southampton on 23 December 2006?

455. Which Blackburn Rovers 'keeper equalised for them in the last minute of their Premier League game at The Valley against Charlton Athletic on 21 February 2004, only to concede an even later goal and lose the match 3-2?

456. Which Spurs goalkeeper scored with a long clearance against Manchester United in the 1967 Charity Shield at Old Trafford?

457. The 'keeper who conceded that goal was, remarkably, United's joint-top goalscorer for two months of the 1973-74 season with two penalties. Who was he?

458. Who became the first goalkeeper to score in the Premier League when he did so for Aston Villa against Everton on 20 October 2001?

459. Which two 'Steves', both of whom played in goal in a 1980s FA Cup final, have scored a goal in the course of their careers?

460. Which blind rhythm and blues artist nevertheless managed to find the net as a goalkeeper while appearing in the East Fife side that won 2-0 at Stranraer on 28 February 1990? He probably told the other 'keeper he was 'Born to Lose'!

47 GOALSCORING HEROES

461. Who scored a Premier League hat-trick in less than three minutes in the first half of the Southampton v Aston Villa game on 16 May 2015?

462. Which player holds the Premier League record for headed goals with a total of 53 to his name?

463. Who scored four goals after coming on as a substitute when Manchester United won 8-1 at Nottingham Forest in the 1998-99 season?

464. Who scored 21 goals in four cup competitions in the 1965-66 season?

465. Charlie Adam holds the Premier League record for a long-distance goal with his effort from 66 yards for Stoke City at Chelsea, but which player currently has two goals in the top six long-distance goals?

466. In the post-Second World War era, which three Liverpool players have topped the goalscorers' list in a season that takes in all four divisions?

467. Who is the only post-Second World War player to score more than 30 top-flight goals in three successive years?

468. Who was the first man since the arrival of the Premier League to score more than 20 goals in five consecutive seasons?

469. Jimmy Greaves scored on his debuts for all four clubs he played for. Who were they?

470. Only one man scored more League goals in English football than Jimmy, and he did so for WBA, Fulham, Leicester City and Shrewsbury Town between 1947 and 1965. Who was he?

GROUNDS (BUILT POST-SECOND WORLD WAR) 48

471. A cryptic one to start with: which new 1997 Lancastrian ground could be said to have been named after Aidan O'Brien and John Gosden from the world of horse racing?

472. Which new northern ground, also from 1997, has, after translation, broadly the same name as Benfica's ground?

473. Which new ground of 1994 had a number in its name?

474. Which new ground that opened in 2012 borrowed its name from 'the big apple'?

475. Which 2001 new ground included in its title a reference to the club's original name of 1885?

476. Which was the earliest ground built post-Second World War that is still in use today?

477. Which southern ground that opened in 1990 was, three years later, sharing its name with the club's new manager?

478. Which new ground in 2016, if there was any justice in the world, should have been called The Bobby Moore Stadium?

479. Which new ground of 2002 was named after a bag of crisps?

480. Wigan Athletic's new 1999 ground, originally known as the JJB Stadium, was renamed the DW Stadium to reflect which man's colossal contribution to the club?

49 GROUNDS (GONE BUT NOT FORGOTTEN)

481. Which ground that closed in 2006 saw 13 League titles won on it?

482. Which ground that was the venue for three successive titles in the 1920s was the only ground that contained the name of a rival club in its name? It went in 1994.

483. Which was the first ground built post-Second World War, from 1946, that was demolished in the early years of this century?

484. Which ground that disappeared in 2003 still holds the attendance record for a club ground in both League and cup football, set in the 1940s and 1930s respectively?

485. Which two grounds that were used during the 1966 World Cup series had time called upon them in the 1990s?

486. Which ground that became defunct in 1997 saw Stanley Matthews dance down its wings both before and after the Second World War?

487. Another sport besides football was involved in the naming of which Midlands club's ground that saw two titles won on it before its closure in 1997?

488. Also closing its doors in 1997 was a ground that was the scene of a footballing tragedy that killed 33 spectators through overcrowding in an FA Cup tie in 1946. Which ground was it?

489. Which national stadium and home to the only side to take the FA Cup out of England closed in 2009?

490. Which ground with its much-loved Milton Road End met its date with the bulldozer in 2001?

GROUNDS IN GENERAL 50

491. The last European Cup Winners' Cup final in 1999 was played between Lazio and Real Mallorca on which English club ground?
A. Elland Road B. Old Trafford C. Villa Park D. White Hart Lane

492. Which Scottish club ground references another sport in its name?

493. Which four English grounds experimented with plastic pitches during the 1980s?

494. The FA Cup semi-final in April 1988 that featured Wimbledon and Luton Town produced the smallest crowd for that stage of the competition in its history. On which ground did 25,963 people assemble for the match, and on which ground was that record broken by the 17,987 who watched Manchester United and Crystal Palace replay their 1995 semi-final?

495. Which four current club grounds have been used for an FA Cup final or replay?

496. A legendary ground was bulldozed in 2006, but within a decade a new club came into League football with a ground that had the same name as the now defunct one. By what name were the two grounds known?

497. Which two grounds, geographically about as far apart as you can get in England, nevertheless share a name?

498. Which two grounds are situated closest to each other in English football?

499. In 1993 a club moved from its old ground but kept the ground's name, merely adding the prefix 'New'. Over time the prefix was discarded so it now has its old name restored. Which ground is described?

500. The first British ground to host a European Cup final was also a club ground. Which ground was it and which club played their home games there?

51 HAT-TRICKS

501. Which England international centre forward scored a hat-trick inside nine minutes of his Swansea City debut in a 5-1 win over Leeds United on the opening day of the 1981-82 season?

502. When this teenager scored a hat-trick on his Southampton debut against Arsenal in 1988, he broke a 30-year record as the youngest scorer of a top-flight hat-trick. Who was he and whose record did he beat?

503. Juan Seminario is the only South American to score a hat-trick against England, doing so on 17 May 1959 when which country won 4-1?

504. Robbie Fowler had a sensational four and a half minutes at Anfield in the 1994-95 season, during which he found the net three times against which club?

505. When England beat the USA 10-0 away on 27 May 1964, a player from both Merseyside clubs contributed a hat-trick, the man from the red half grabbing four goals. Who were the two men, one of whom was making his international debut?

506. Which Dutchman scored a hat-trick against England at the 1988 Euros to ruin Peter Shilton's 100th appearance in England's goal?

507. When George Camsell hit 59 goals for Middlesbrough in 1926-27, he must have thought he'd be long dead before anyone got near his total. Cue Dixie Dean reaching 60 the following season, with a final-day hat-trick to celebrate the title in a 3-3 draw against which club?

508. Bill Townley in 1890 and Jimmy Logan in 1894 were the only two men to score a hat-trick in an FA Cup final in the 19th century. Which two clubs were they playing for?

509. What strange experience have Brian Clark of Bournemouth, Jack Dodds of Lincoln City, David Herd of Manchester United and Alvin Martin of West Ham United all shared?

510. Geoff Hurst, Gary Lineker and Harry Kane have all scored England hat-tricks in World Cup competitions. Who were the three beaten countries?

INTERNATIONAL CAPS   52

511. A Welshman who won 75 caps between 1986 and 2001 is the only player to represent one of the four home nations while at ten different clubs. Who was he?

512. Which player remained unbeaten in his first 21 England internationals between 2000 and 2003?

513. Which England international capped 62 times for his country between 1990 and 1996 gained those caps while with two English and three Italian clubs?

514. Who went one better where Italian clubs were concerned by playing 72 times for the Republic of Ireland between 1975 and 1990 while with four teams from that country?

515. Between 1964 and 1977, George Best won 37 Northern Ireland caps, the vast majority while with Manchester United. With which other club was he capped for his country?

516. Arguably the two greatest Scottish forwards since the Second World War, Denis Law and Kenny Dalglish played in a combined total of 157 games for their country and ended up with the same goals total. What was it?

517. Goalkeepers Peter Shilton of England, Jim Leighton of Scotland, Neville Southall of Wales, Pat Jennings of Northern Ireland and Shay Given of the Republic of Ireland were the recipients of 561 caps between them. Which of the five had the most?

518. Which player who gained 49 caps for Wales between 2002 and 2014 received the first of them with a Welsh club and later received caps while at three London clubs?

519. Which Republic of Ireland international winger made exactly 100 appearances for his country between 1998 and 2012?

520. Five 'Wrights' have been capped post-Second World War by England. Ian Wright, Mark Wright and Tommy Wright constitute the middle three where caps are concerned, but who, with 105, has the most, and who, with just two, has the least?

53 KEEP ON KEEPING ON!

521. Which England international goalkeeper has played in the Premier League with his surname on the back and front of his jersey?

522. On the afternoon of 26 November 1958, a goalkeeper played for Wales in a 2-2 draw against England at Villa Park, before racing back to Highbury to represent Arsenal in their 3-1 win over Juventus in an evening friendly. Who was he?

523. Which two post-Second World War England 'keepers, one with 75 caps to his name and the other with just one, won the Grand National in 1882 and 1905 respectively?

524. He did handstands in his goalmouth before games, played nearly 800 times for 20 clubs between 1968 and 1996 and turned out in the Premier League in his forties. Who was he?

525. Which Polish 'keeper dubbed 'The Clown' by Brian Clough had a blinder in a World Cup qualifier against England at Wembley in October 1973, killing the home nation's hopes of going to the 1994 World Cup?

526. I was at Elm Park on the night of 31 August 1962 when Reading's 'keeper injured his hand against Halifax Town and then went up front to score twice in a 4-2 win. Who was he?

527. Who were the first two goalkeepers to play in successive post-Second World War FA Cup finals?

528. Rob Green was capped for England while at Norwich City and West Ham United. If you put another post-war England 'keeper and FA Cup winner in front of his surname, you produce a London Underground station, and if you put another FA Cup-winning goalkeeper's surname behind his surname, you end up with a rock group! Which two 'keepers do you need to make this happen?

529. Which legendary 'keeper who weighed well over 20 stone played in three FA Cup finals for Sheffield United in 1899, 1901 and 1902?

530. Who is the only goalkeeper with two Zs in his surname to play in an FA Cup final?

LEAGUE CUP 1960-1999 – CLUBS 54

Because it has had numerous sponsors over the years, I will use the original name 'League Cup' in all the sections involved.

531. Which club failed to win the trophy in the first 20 years of its history and then promptly won it four times in a row?

532. Which club who have never played top-flight football nevertheless figured in the first final in 1961, when they contrived to lose a two-goal lead from the first leg to Aston Villa?

533. Which team lost consecutive League Cup finals in the 1990s before winning it for the first time in 2004?

534. Who were the only side to win the League Cup in the 1970s, 1980s and 1990s?

535. The first six finals were over two legs, with the 1967 event being the first single-match Wembley final. A Third Division outfit came from two goals down in that final to beat their top-flight opponents 3-2. Which two clubs fought it out?

536. 1976 provided the first occasion when two clubs who had already met each other in an FA Cup final played each other in the League Cup final as well. The FA Cup final they had contested took place 21 years before. Who were the two teams?

537. Which club who have won nothing else in their history have twice been successful in this competition, in 1962 and 1985?

538. Which two clubs who both won the League Cup in the 1980s later experienced non-League football?

539. Which London club have reached two League Cup finals without taking the trophy?

540. In 1993 the FA Cup final and the League Cup final were between the same two teams for the first time. Which two clubs contested them?

55 LEAGUE CUP 1960-1999 – PLAYERS

541. Four members of England's World Cup-winning team of 1966 had previously appeared in a League Cup final. Who was the only one of the four to appear in two before that World Cup?

542. When Swindon Town created a big splash by beating Arsenal 3-1 in the 1969 final, which player scored two of those three goals from the wing?

543. In this period five players scored from the penalty spot in a League Cup final. Chronologically, they played for Chelsea, Nottingham Forest, West Ham United, Nottingham Forest again and Aston Villa. Can you name the five?

544. Which goalkeeper played for Liverpool in the 1981 final and against them in the 1982 final?

545. Who scored Arsenal's winning goal in the 1993 final, only to have his greatest moment in football ruined by being badly injured in the after-match celebrations?

546. Which Spurs player was sent off in the 1999 final against Leicester City after being wound up like a watch by Robbie Savage?

547. Which goalkeeper was twice a loser in a League Cup final, first with Luton Town in 1989 and then with Manchester United two years later?

548. The 1977 final between Aston Villa and Everton took three games and extra time before it was settled 3-2 in Villa's favour by a stunning 35-yard effort from their centre half. Who was he?

549. Which Liverpool defender scored for them in both the 1981 and 1983 finals?

550. Two members of the losing Stoke City side in the 1964 final had played in earlier FA Cup finals for Lancastrian rivals – one for Blackburn Rovers in 1960 and the other for Burnley in 1962. Who were they?

LEAGUE CUP 2000-2022 – CLUBS 56

551. In this period Liverpool have won the trophy three times through the penalty shoot-out route. Their wins came in 2001, 2012 and 2022. Which three clubs lost to them in this manner, the last in highly amusing circumstances due to a certain goalkeeper's involvement?

552. The 2013 final saw two teams making their League Cup final debuts and produced the biggest winning margin of any such final. Which two clubs contested it?

553. Who are the only club in this period to make an appearance in the final and then end up playing non-League football?

554. Manchester City won the trophy four years in a row between 2018 and 2021. Three of their wins came against London clubs. Whom did they beat in the other one?

555. Two clubs that begin with the same letter had both played in and lost a League Cup final between 1960 and 1999. Now, in this period, they repeated the pattern in 2014 and 2017. Who were the two clubs?

556. Which London club has appeared in three finals in this period without winning the League Cup?

557. In this century two clubs have beaten and lost to Chelsea in a League Cup final. Who are they?

558. Two clubs from the same city played in consecutive finals in 2010 and 2011. One of them lost the first final but the other produced a shock win in the second. Who were the two clubs?

559. Besides Liverpool and Manchester City, who have won five between them, who is the only other side to win the League Cup in a penalty shoot-out this century?

560. Three Lancastrian towns have appeared in a League Cup final between 2000 and 2022, one winning the trophy and the other two going home empty-handed. Who are the three?

57 LEAGUE CUP 2000-2022 – PLAYERS

561. The Chelsea v Arsenal League Cup final of 2007 erupted in a brawl six minutes from the end, and three players – two from Arsenal, one from Chelsea – got their marching orders. Who were they?

562. In the 2002 final, fans held up a banner that proclaimed 'Cole strikes in the valleys'. It proved to be prescient. Why?

563. Which player scored for and against Manchester United in a League Cup final this century?

564. Which goalkeeper was sent off in the 58th minute of the 2013 League Cup final?

565. Spurs lost the 2015 final to Chelsea and the 2021 final to Manchester City. One man played for them in the first final and managed them in the second. Who was he?

566. Who scored both Leicester City goals when they won the first League Cup of this period in 2000?

567. When Liverpool won the penalty shoot-out that decided the 2012 final, two cousins – one for Liverpool, the other for their opponents – missed from the spot. What was their collective surname?

568. Who was the only player with a 'z' in his name to score in a League Cup final for Chelsea in this period when he did so in the 2005 final?

569. When Manchester United won, slightly fortunately, the 2017 final, their 3-2 win was achieved by two goals by Zlatan Ibrahimovic that sandwiched one by which other United player?

570. Which Middlesbrough player with two figures from the Bible in his name took just two minutes to find the net in the 2004 League Cup final?

FOOTBALL LEAGUE TITLES 1888-1939   58

571. Which club won the Football League in the first two seasons of its formation but have not won it since?

572. Which club in 1894-95 became the first to win the League on three occasions?

573. Which club won the Football League five times in seven years between 1893 and 1900?

574. Which club won the League three times in five seasons between 1904 and 1909?

575. In the first two seasons back after the First World War, in 1919-20 and 1920-21, there were two new names on the list of winners of the League title, one from the Midlands and the other from Lancashire. Who were they?

576. Which club that already had five FA Cup wins to its name landed the Football League title in 1911-12 and 1913-14?

577. By winning the League title in 1914-15 and again in 1938-39, this club held the trophy through two world wars. Who were they?

578. Which Yorkshire club were never out of the top three in six consecutive years in the 1920s, claiming three successive titles into the bargain?

579. Which club started its League title-winning spree in the 1930-31 season and by the end of the decade had five to their name?

580. Which club won the title four times in this period, the first two arriving in 1902-03 and 1903-04 under their original name, and then in 1928-29 and 1929-30 under their current name?

59 FOOTBALL LEAGUE TITLES 1946-1992

581. The first post-Second World War season was badly weather-disrupted and went on until June. Which club, in losing their last game at Sheffield United, ended up outside the top three when victory would have provided them with the only Football League title in their history?

582. Which club who had no League titles before and have had none since stormed to successive victories in 1948-49 and 1949-50?

583. Which club in 1950-51 became the first post-Second World War team to win the Football League after promotion into the top flight the previous season?

584. Which club were runners-up in the League in four of the first five seasons after the Second World War, before finally landing the title in 1951-52?

585. Which club that have gone on to collect a few more along the way won their first League title in their golden jubilee season of 1954-55?

586. Which club who won the League in 1980-81 for the seventh time were ending a drought of over 70 years?

587. For how many years in a row in the 1980s did the Football League Championship trophy reside on Merseyside?

588. When Derby County won the League title in 1971-72, they had finished their League programme and were waiting on one result that would decide where the trophy would end up. Which two sides were involved in that game?

589. Which two clubs, one in 1961-62 and the other in 1977-78, won the League in their first season in the top flight after achieving promotion the previous season?

590. Which other club besides Manchester United won three titles in the 1950s?

PREMIER LEAGUE TITLES 1992-2022   60

591. Who are the only two Premier League-winning clubs to have met each other in a play-off final at Wembley?

592. Who are the only club to win the Premier League on goal difference?

593. Who are the only club to finish as runners-up in the Premier League in three consecutive seasons?

594. Who is the only non-European manager to win the Premier League?

595. At one point in Premier League history, only one club stood between the Manchester clubs keeping the trophy in their city for a ten-year period. Which club was it?

596. In the first three years of the Premier League, the three sides that finished third all began with the same letter. Who were the three?

597. The gap between the lowest and highest points total to win the Premier League is 25. What are the two points totals and to which clubs do they belong?

598. Who are the only side to win the Premier League undefeated over their 38 matches, and in which season did they do so?

599. Which club failed to win the Premier League despite the champions in a particular season losing four times as many games as they did?

600. Which four clubs that begin with the same letter have experienced both Premier League football and fourth-tier football in this period?

61 LINKS

601. What links Jermain Defoe, Paul Gascoigne, Jimmy Greaves and Gareth Southgate?

602. Tom Finney, Danny Blanchflower and Jack Charlton shared 167 caps between them. What else did they share?

603. Apart from their Manchester United connection, what else links Ryan Giggs, Teddy Sheringham and Gordon Strachan?

604. What links Otman Bakkal of PSV Eindhoven and Morocco, Branislav Ivanović of Chelsea and Serbia and Giorgio Chiellini of Juventus and Italy?

605. In the first 20 or so years after the Second World War, what did John Charles, Ray Crawford, Roger Hunt and Charlie Wayman do that nobody else managed to?

606. What links Marcel Desailly, Gustavo Dezotti, Johnny Heitinga, Pedro Monzón and Zinedine Zidane?

607. What links Bobby Johnstone of Manchester City, Bobby Smith of Spurs, Freddie Ljungberg of Arsenal and Didier Drogba of Chelsea?

608. What links Bradford City, Cardiff City, Coventry City, Leicester City and Manchester City?

609. What links Bury, Nottingham Forest, Old Etonians, Portsmouth, Preston North End and Sunderland where the FA Cup is concerned?

610. What links Nottingham Forest players Archie Gemmill, Larry Lloyd, John McGovern and Peter Withe and separates them from the other Forest players who won the Football League in the 1970s?

LOCAL DERBIES PART 1   62

611. Why was the 1990-91 season unique concerning matches between Arsenal and Spurs?

612. A club came close to being the first of the 20th century to do the FA Cup and Football League 'double' when they took the FA Cup in 1954 and finished second in the League to their close rivals. Which two teams were involved?

613. The highest number of goals in a Liverpool v Everton derby came at Anfield on 11 February 1933, when 11 were scored. How did the game end up? A. 6-5 to Liverpool B. 7-4 to Liverpool C. 8-3 to Liverpool D. 9-2 to Liverpool?

614. Which local rivals met each other in the 1963 League Cup final over two legs?

615. When Manchester City and Manchester United met on 22 September 2013, a game that City won 4-1 at the Etihad Stadium, it was the first time in 26 years that the derby had two new managers facing each other. Who were they?

616. The Celtic v Rangers derby puts all the others in the shade and rarely disappoints despite the declining number of Glaswegians in the contest. One of the most exciting came at Ibrox Park on 22 March 1986 and ended all square with what score?

617. On 5 December 1908 one club won 9-1 on the ground of their close rivals, but at the season's end they were in third place and the team they humiliated in front of their own fans were champions. Which two clubs were involved?

618. The 1992-93 season produced two FA Cup semi-final derbies. Which four clubs contested them?

619. Which intense rivalry has been given the title 'The M23 Derby'?

620. Two much-loved players, John Atyeo and Geoff Bradford, were major figures in the 1950s in which local derby?

65

63 LOCAL DERBIES PART 2

621. Which two clubs from the same city met each other in the 1896 Scottish Cup final and then had to wait 116 years before the chance came again?

622. One club joined Division Three at the start of the 1920-21 season and seven years later their close rivals from the same county played their first game in Division Three South, in which they played out a 1-1 draw at home to that first club. Who were the two teams?

623. Which two clubs from the same city played each other for the last time in the Football League on 12 February 1994?

624. In which local derby did Paul Gascoigne head a dramatic 89th-minute leveller on 29 November 1992?

625. Which two teams from the same city contested the Scottish League Cup final in 1981?

626. Which two deadly rivals met in the 2015 Championship play-off semi-final, with the winner going on to reach the Premier League at the expense of Middlesbrough in the final at Wembley?

627. Which defender in the 1963-64 season became the only man before or since to play in the Football League for Arsenal against Spurs and for Spurs against Arsenal in the same season?

628. Manchester United beat Manchester City 1-0 in the League Cup in 1974-75. Why was the game unique among Manchester derbies?

629. Stanley Matthews and Jackie Mudie were members of Blackpool's FA Cup-winning side of 1953, and both of them either played or managed on both sides of which derby that didn't involve Blackpool?

630. The 1959-60 Football League champions had their chance to be the first 20th century club to do the 'double' but lost a thrilling FA Cup quarter-final to their neighbours in a replay after holding a 3-0 lead towards the end of the first game. Which two clubs were involved?

MANAGERS: BRITISH 64

631. Before the First World War, Tom Watson won the Football League as a manager with Sunderland and Liverpool. Who were the next two men to win the League with two different clubs?

632. He played for one university city and managed another, led a team to two FA Cup wins in the 1980s, and then in the next decade won the League Cup with two more clubs. Who was he?

633. Who were the first two clubs on Alex Ferguson's impressive managerial CV?

634. Which manager won the FA Cup with one northern club in 1992 before adding the League Cup with another northern club exactly ten years later?

635. As a player he was in consecutive FA Cup finals for Manchester City in the 1950s before winning two League titles, two Fairs Cups, an FA Cup and a League Cup with another club over the next two decades. Who was he?

636. Who managed the first club to do the Football League and FA Cup 'double' in the 20th century?

637. Which manager who has led teams in Europe and won the FA Cup didn't have the greatest introduction to his managerial career when he lost his very first game in charge 9-0 at Lincoln City?

638. Who was the last Englishman to be in charge of a League-winning side?

639. Bill Shankly became something of a secular saint at Anfield, but he came up the hard way as a player in the inter-war years and had a tough start to his managerial career at which four northern English clubs before reaching Liverpool in 1959?

640. Two Scots, Jock Stein and Matt Busby, were the first two British men to manage European Cup winners, and no Londoner has done so. Who came the closest when his Barcelona team lost a penalty shoot-out to Steaua Bucharest in 1986?

65 MANAGERS FOREIGN

641. Who was the first foreign manager to win the Champions League with a British club?

642. Who lasted just 85 days when he became the first American manager of a Premier League club after taking charge of Swansea City in 2016?

643. Which foreign manager presided over wins in three competitions for his club in 2001?

644. Manchester United had no manager from outside Great Britain and Ireland in the first 122 years of their existence, but have more than made up for it with five in the last eight years. Who are they?

645. Which three foreign managers have taken English clubs to the coveted League and FA Cup 'double'?

646. Who became West Ham United's first foreign manager in 2008?

647. In this century to 2023, Chelsea have employed five managers whose surnames end with the same letter. Who are they?

648. Who was the first non-British manager in Spurs' history?

649. Everton were 125 years into their history before they employed a manager from outside Britain and Ireland. Who was he?

650. Aston Villa were earlier on the scene than most when it came to hiring foreign managers when they gave an opportunity to which man in 1990?

NICKNAMES

66

651. Which two English clubs share the same first letter of their names, the same colours and the same nickname?

652. We all know who the Red Devils are, but who are the Green Devils?

653. What do Hearts, Everton, Bournemouth, Morecambe and Bolton Wanderers have in common?

654. Which two clubs share the nickname 'The Latics'?

655. Why might a match between Hull City and Millwall get a little bit out of hand?

656. Likewise, if Huddersfield Town and Sunderland went head-to-head?

657. Which three clubs have all been known as The Robins?

658. What links Luton Town, Northampton Town and Yeovil Town apart from all being 'Towns'?

659. Which two London clubs share the first letter of their names and their nickname, and met each other in the FA Cup fourth round in 2019?

660. In a competition between Bradford City, Brighton & Hove Albion, Cardiff City, Crystal Palace, Norwich City, Sheffield Wednesday, Tottenham Hotspur and West Bromwich Albion, who would you expect to emerge triumphant through the feathers and mayhem?

67 OCCUPATIONS

All the players in the answers have occupations for surnames.

661. Which stalwart Welsh international centre half played more than 250 League games for Swansea in two spells that sandwiched over 100 games at Middlesbrough and Swindon Town in a career that played out between 1955 and 1970?

662. Who played in goal for Oxford United when they secured their only major trophy by winning the 1986 League Cup final against Queens Park Rangers?

663. In the early 1960s, Spurs had one of these at right back and rivals Arsenal had one of their own at centre forward. Who were the two players?

664. Defences were all at sea against which Ipswich Town cup winner in 1978?

665. This Leeds United enforcer was appropriately named as he went looking for his prey, which included Peter Osgood and, on one memorable occasion, Francis Lee. Who was he?

666. Which defender played more than 350 League games for Bournemouth between 2012 and 2022?

667. Which Ipswich Town player was famously pictured in an appropriately bloody England shirt doing battle for his country?

668. This wing half was a member of the Burnley side in the 1962 FA Cup final and also told his story in Chaucer's Canterbury Tales and much later in Procol Harum's A Whiter Shade of Pale. Who was he?

669. They probably 'rolled out the barrel' when celebrating his goal that won the League Cup for Leeds United in 1968. Who was he?

670. If you are organising a large function that includes dining, you will need this goalkeeper who played over 250 League games for Blackpool from the late 1950s to the mid-1960s and also gained five England caps. Who was he?

ODD ONE OUT

68

671. Charlton Athletic – Crystal Palace – Fulham – West Ham United
Three of those London clubs have twice been promoted to the top flight via the play-offs, but one of them has done so on four occasions. Which one is it?

672. Argentina – Brazil – Chile – Paraguay – Uruguay
Which one of these South American countries has never played in a World Cup semi-final?

673. Atletico Madrid – Borussia Dortmund – Marseille – PSV Eindhoven – Red Star Belgrade – Steaua Bucharest
Which one these clubs has never won the European Cup/Champions League?

674. Cardiff City – Hull City – Millwall – Portsmouth – Southampton – Stoke City – Tottenham Hotspur – Wigan Athletic
Which one of these clubs hasn't played in an FA Cup final this century?

675. Bolton Wanderers – Burnley – Preston North End – Wolves
Who are the only one of the four not to have won the old First, Second, Third and Fourth Divisions?

676. Bloomfield Road – Deepdale – Ewood Park – Turf Moor
Which Lancastrian ground have England not played on?

677. 1986 World Cup quarter-finals: Argentina v England Brazil v France – Spain v Belgium – West Germany v Mexico
Which game is the odd one out and why?

678. John Aldridge – Eden Hazard – Glenn Hoddle – Arnold Mühren – Ruud van Nistelrooy
Which of the five is the odd man out and why?

679. Aberdeen – Hearts – Hibernian – Queen's Park
Which is the only one of the four to have reached double figures in Scottish Cup final wins?

680. Brighton & Hove Albion – Leicester City – Manchester City Middlesbrough – Portsmouth – Wigan Athletic
What do those six clubs have in common, which is the odd one out, and why?

69 ONE-CAP WONDERS PART 1

All the following players appeared once for England.

681. His earlier Everton namesake received 72 caps in his overall career but this defender had to make do with just one, which came his way in 2001. Who was he?

682. Which rock at the heart of Stoke City's defence managed just one England cap in 2013?

683. This big guy with a big character was a central defender with several clubs, and his only cap came while with Liverpool in 1995. Who was he?

684. Injury brought a premature end to this centre forward's career, and his only game for his country came while at West Ham United in 2008. Who was he?

685. Which combative midfielder, who was known for the odd clash with opponents, authorities and sometimes his teammates, received his only cap while at Manchester City in 2007?

686. This man turned out more times for Spurs than anyone else in their history, but his sole England call-up came in 1982. Who was he?

687. Which Everton player was one third of their finest ever midfield and deserved more than his one cap, which came in 1971?

688. This scorer of an FA Cup-winning goal with another club eventually received his solitary cap while playing at Derby County in 1977. Who was he?

689. Which forward gained his only cap while at Aston Villa in 1975 and later went on to manage that club?

690. Which winger left Bolton Wanderers to go north to Celtic, gaining his only England cap while playing Scottish football in 2004?

ONE-CAP WONDERS PART 2   70

691. We ended the last section with a player who moved to Scotland to gain an England cap, so let's start this one with another who received his sole cap in 1991 with Glasgow Rangers after playing in England with Aston Villa and Liverpool. Who was he?
692. Two Manchester United players who were in the Munich air disaster both played once for England. A stalwart defender who survived and carried on playing received his in 1955, while the other, who was capped in 1957, was a left winger who sadly did not survive. Who were the two players?
693. The winning goal of the 1966 FA Cup final came when a Sheffield Wednesday player misjudged a ball and an Everton player ran through to make it 3-2. Both men gained just one England cap. Who were they?
694. Two men who share a surname received their sole England caps in 1960 and 1971, the first as a centre half for West Ham United and the second as a record-breaking goalscorer for West Bromwich Albion. Who were the two players?
695. Burnley's number 2 and number 11 in the 1962 FA Cup final against Spurs both played once for England. Who were they?
696. Which striker did his international career few favours when he fell out with Glenn Hoddle, his only cap coming in 1997 while with Blackburn Rovers?
697. Which inside forward who played more than 400 times for Sheffield Wednesday and scored their consolation goal in a 1960 FA Cup semi-final gained his only England cap in 1962?
698. Which superb midfielder won his England cap in 1963 while at Everton, but ruined any chance of gaining more after being banned from the game?
699. Which two Arsenal players with names beginning with J were capped once each for England, the first in 2003 and the second ten years later?
700. Add one letter to the middle of the surname of a Norwich City player capped once in 1976 and you produce a Leeds United player also capped once in 2003. Who are the two players?

71 ORIGINS

Here is a set of ten fixtures using the clubs' original names. Can you place the 20 modern club names in the right spot on the fixture list?

701. Thames Ironworks v Newton Heath

702. Pine Villa v Shaddongate United

703. St Domingo v St Mary's

704. West Herts v Thornhill United

705. Headington United v Ardwick

706. New Brompton v Singers FC

707. Black Arabs v Dial Square

708. Small Heath Alliance v St Jude's

709. St Luke's v Belmont

710. Christ Church v Stanley

Arsenal	Newcastle United
Birmingham City	Oldham Athletic
Bolton Wanderers	Oxford United
Bristol Rovers	QPR
Carlisle United	Rotherham United
Coventry City	Southampton
Everton	Tranmere Rovers
Gillingham	Watford
Manchester City	West Ham United
Manchester United	Wolves

OUR NAME'S ON THE CUP   72

The following FA Cup finals were characterised by having a player on each side with the same surname. Can you place the surnames below in the appropriate finals?

711. The Wanderers v The Royal Engineers – 1878

712. Bury v Southampton – 1900

713. Bury v Derby County – 1903

714. Bolton Wanderers v Portsmouth – 1929

715. Spurs v Leicester City – 1961

716. Everton v Sheffield Wednesday – 1966

717. Liverpool v Newcastle United – 1974

718. Liverpool v Sunderland – 1992

719. Portsmouth v Cardiff City – 2008

720. Arsenal v Aston Villa – 2015

Cook
Johnson
Lindsay
Norman
Richards

Rush
Sanchez
Smith
Wood
Young

73 OWN GOALS

721. In the first post-Second World War FA Cup final of 1946, some strange things happened. Firstly, the ball burst, and then for the first time in an FA Cup final a player scored for both sides while turning out for Charlton Athletic against Derby County. Who was he?

722. In 1985 the League Cup final was decided in favour of Norwich City through a Gordon Chisholm own goal. Which club was he representing?

723. In the 1980s there were two instances of a player scoring for both clubs in an FA Cup final and Spurs were involved in both; first when a Manchester City man did so against them in 1981 and then when one of their own players repeated the trick against Coventry City in 1987. Who were the two players?

724. In Aston Villa's 2-2 away draw with Leicester City in March 1976, one of their players scored all four goals. Who was he?
A. Frank Carrodus B. John Gidman C. Ray Graydon D. Chris Nicholl

725. For which club was Mick McGrath playing when he scored an own goal against Wolves in the 1960 FA Cup final?

726. Whose own goal in the 2006 FA Cup final would have brought a smile to the face of Gary Neville?

727. Five months later that smile would have disappeared when his back pass while playing away to Croatia rolled past the England 'keeper's air shot to put him on the scorers' sheet. Who was the goalkeeper?

728. In the Liverpool v Leeds United game at Anfield in December 1967, whose own goal produced a rendition of Des O'Connor's Careless Hands from the Kop?

729. In the second leg of the 1989 UEFA Cup final against Stuttgart a player scored a goal against his own Italian side, who still went on to win the trophy. What was odd was that the player and his team shared the same name. What was it?

730. The most costly own goal of all! Which Colombian player was murdered upon returning home after his own goal against the USA helped eliminate his country from the 1994 World Cup?

PENALTY! PART 1   74

731. Which classy Danish international scored a hat-trick of penalties for Liverpool in a League Cup tie against Coventry at Anfield in November 1986?

732. Which southern English club managed to miss seven successive penalties in the early 1990s? A. Gillingham B. Portsmouth C. Southend United D. Swindon Town

733. Only one World Cup final has produced a goal from the penalty spot for both teams. What was the year and which two countries were involved?

734. In 2004-05, Crystal Palace were relegated from the Premier League despite which player scoring 11 penalties for them over the season?

735. Which player missed just one of the 49 penalties he took in his career?

736. Who was the first post-Second World War England player to score twice from the penalty spot in a World Cup competition?

737. Who scored from the spot for Ipswich Town in the first leg of the UEFA Cup final against AZ Alkmaar at Portman Road in 1981, when they went on to win it under Bobby Robson? A. Paul Mariner B. Arnold Mühren C. Frans Thijssen D. John Wark

738. Not only did the 1994 World Cup final, when Brazil beat Italy, end with a penalty shoot-out, but it started with one as well, staged for a well-known singer. Unfortunately, she botched the kick and the makeshift net collapsed in an organisers' own goal! Who was she?

739. Arsenal, leading 2-1 in the 1988 League Cup final, were awarded a penalty but eventually lost the game 3-2 to Luton Town after missing it. Which unfortunate Gunner failed from the spot?

740. Manchester United were the first club in English football to win a game with a penalty shoot-out when they beat Hull City by that method to take the Watney Cup in 1970. Who became the first player to score in a penalty shoot-out?
A. George Best B. Bobby Charlton C. Brian Kidd D. Denis Law

75 PENALTY! PART 2

741. The first penalty to be scored in an English League game came on 14 September 1891 and contributed to Wolves' 5-0 win over Accrington, who had the 'Stanley' bit added that year. The scorer's name was John and he shared his surname with a Conservative Party leader. Who was he?
A. Baldwin B. Cameron C. Heath D. Johnson

742. Which club did Eintracht Frankfurt beat 5-4 in a penalty shoot-out after a 1-1 draw in Seville in 2022, to lift the Europa League trophy?

743. On Easter Monday 1989, a record five penalties were awarded in a Division Two match between two clubs who don't like each other very much. Who were they?

744. Why did Ray Graydon not care overmuch that he missed his penalty against Norwich City when playing for Aston Villa in the 1975 League Cup final?

745. When his club won 7-2 away from home at Gillingham in League One on 29 January 2022, Cameron Brannagan created a new record for penalties scored in a game. How many did he score and who was he playing for?

746. Which Manchester City man who topped the Division One scoring charts in the 1971-72 season scored 13 of his 33 goals from the penalty spot, without missing one?

747. Which club left Wembley in 2019 having won the Football League Trophy by beating Sunderland on penalties, but left the same stage the following year less happy, after losing to Salford City by the same process in the same event?

748. Which English club in 1991 became the most westerly one to win promotion through a penalty shoot-out when they clambered out of Division Four by that method, beating Blackpool after a 2-2 draw at Wembley?

749. In which year was the last time that both sides scored from the penalty spot in an FA Cup final?

750. Which two clubs were playing when the FA Cup final was decided by penalties for the first time?

PLACES OF INTEREST   76

All the answers are players whose surnames relate to geographical locations.

751. Alex Ferguson's purchase of Eric Cantona from Leeds United came about partly because which Manchester United forward who shares his name with a capital city had broken his leg?

752. Which English county with his cross helped set up Trevor Brooking's winning goal for West Ham United against Arsenal in the 1980 FA Cup final?

753. Which town in south Wales has played in more Premier League games than anyone else?

754. The town in Iowa where jazz great Bix Beiderbecke was born is also the name of a forward Manchester United bought from Nottingham Forest in the mid-1980s who could have figured in our 'One-cap wonders' section. Who was he?

755. Which city scored for Sheffield United in an FA Cup semi-final at Wembley in 1993?

756. Eric Clapton's birthplace is the name of one of the players that won the Premier League in 1994-95 with Blackburn Rovers. Who is he?

757. Which area of London scored for England after just 37 seconds of an international against South Africa in Durban on 22 May 2003?

758. Which Greek island has scored more than 200 League goals this century, the majority of them at Blackburn Rovers and Huddersfield Town?

759. Which town on the border between England and Wales scored seven times when Preston North End set up a record FA Cup victory by beating Hyde 26-0 in October 1887?

760. Which Lancastrian town appropriately played in goal for Blackburn Rovers in the 1960 FA Cup final?

77 PLAY-OFFS 1987-2022

761. Which club, despite losing six successive games on the run-in and going down 2-0 at home to Derby County early on in the semi-final first leg, still managed to get promoted via the play-offs to take their place for the first season of Premier League football in the 1992-93 season?

762. Which two clubs fought out a superb 1998 play-off final which finished 4-4 and was eventually decided by a missed penalty by Michael Gray in the shoot-out?

763. In the 1999 play-off to get out of the third tier of English football, whose dramatic last-minute leveller provided the opportunity for Manchester City to win on penalties, and which club did they beat in heartbreaking fashion?

764. Whose hat-trick for Ipswich Town in the second leg of a 2000 Football League play-off semi-final against Bolton Wanderers set up a winning final over Barnsley that made up for their three consecutive semi-final failures in the play-offs before it?

765. When Bolton Wanderers beat Preston North End 3-0 in the 2001 First Division play-off final, the two managers involved later each managed the same two clubs. Who were the managers and the two clubs they went on to be in charge of?

766. Who scored a hat-trick that included two penalties when Swansea City beat Reading 4-2 in the 2011 play-off final to reach the Premier League?

767. After scoring the winning goal for West Ham United against Preston North End in the 2005 play-off final, who waited another nine years before doing it again for QPR against Derby County in 2014?

768. If you think nine years is a big gap, which player found the net for two clubs over 15 years and in different centuries in the Division One play-offs?

769. What was the score of the second leg of the League One play-off semi-final at the County Ground between Swindon Town and Sheffield United in 2015?

770. Only two play-off finals to get into the top flight have been London derbies. They came in 2004 and 2020. Which four clubs were involved?

PREMIER PUZZLERS 78

The answers are all players who have appeared in the Premier League.

771. If the referee saw him doing this in his own penalty area, this Arsenal defender might well concede a penalty.

772. This much-travelled centre forward who has recently retired has to do this to ensure it's a fair contest when he goes up for a ball with a defender!

773. This goalkeeper could be advertising a removal company or a car manufacturer.

774. Who are the only two months of the year to play in the Premier League?

775. His Tottenham Hotspur squad number really should be 40!

776. If you put together the first name of Chelsea's most iconic player of the last decade with the surname of Spurs' most iconic player of the same period, you produce an early 1960s pop singer. Who is he?

777. It would be asking a lot of any goalkeeper to be infallible but, according to the Catholic church, this Newcastle man must be!

778. All players start out hoping their careers will be like this ex-Watford player who is now at Udinese in Italy. Who is he?

779. Inspector Morse's sidekick dips his digestive in his coffee!

780. Now at Southampton, which ex-Spurs player's name contains the full name of one previous Spurs player and the surname of another?

79 PROMOTION AND RELEGATION PART 1

781. Which original member of the Football League in 1888 went from the top flight to the bottom level of English football in successive seasons in the 1980s?

782. Neil Warnock, with eight to his name, holds the record for managerial promotions. These were achieved at Cardiff City, Huddersfield Town, Notts County, Plymouth Argyle, QPR, Scarborough and Sheffield United. Which was the club among these seven that he took up twice?

783. In the 1950s, which team were known as the 'Yo-yo' club because in that decade they experienced four promotions and three relegations? A. Sheffield United B. Sheffield Wednesday C. Stoke City D. Sunderland

784. Who is the only manager to have won promotion to the Premier League on four occasions?

785. Which club made it from the third tier of English football to the top division through consecutive promotions in 1983-84 and 1984-85?

786. In the first seven seasons of Premier League football starting in 1992-93, which two clubs, one from London and the other from the Midlands, experienced relegation on three occasions each?

787. It was a big shock when the only two members of the original 12 English First Division clubs not to be relegated went together in 1935-36. At that point, combined, their total of League and FA Cup wins stood at 20. Who were the two clubs brought low?

788. Two 'Cities' lead the way where old Division Two titles are concerned, each having six to their name. Who are the two clubs?

789. Brighton & Hove Albion and Scunthorpe United were the last clubs to do what in the 1957-58 season?

790. Who are the only club that has won the English League and many years later had to apply for re-election?

PROMOTION AND RELEGATION PART 2 — 80

791. When this Welsh club were champions of Division Three South in 1938-39, they had to wait until after the war before playing Second Division football in 1946-47. It proved to be a difficult undertaking and they were relegated alongside another Welsh club after conceding a stunning 133 goals. Who were they?

792. Between 1987 and 2022, nearly 40 clubs experienced demotion into the Conference or National League. Which is the only one of them that has won the FA Cup?

793. Since 1998-99, six clubs have reached the Premier League by winning the division below with over 100 points. They were Burnley, Fulham, Leicester City, Newcastle United, Reading and Sunderland. Which one of them scored the most points with a total of 106?

794. The two clubs relegated from the top flight in 1965-66 have had contrasting fortunes. One got into the top flight with three promotions in four seasons and played at that level for just that one season in their history, while the other came back and won the Premier League. Who were the two teams?

795. Who are the only English club to have played all their League games in the top flight for over 100 years?

796. Which club, after winning the 1990 play-off final, were denied access to the First Division through financial irregularities?

797. Which club, bottom of the Premier League before the last day of the 2004-05 season, clambered out of danger by beating Portsmouth, thus relegating Southampton, Norwich City and Crystal Palace?

798. Which club were playing in the Fourth Division in season 1982-83 but were in with the big boys when season 1986-87 began?

799. Who are the only club to achieve promotion to the top flight without losing a game?

800. From the start of the old Second Division in 1892 until the last year of the 'two points for a win' system in 1980-81, who were the only club to be promoted to the First Division with 70 points?

81 QUOTES PART 1

Can you match the quotes with the names at the bottom of the page?

801. 'Someone asked me last week if I missed playing for the Villa. I said "No, I live in one."'

802. 'Cantona gave interviews on art, philosophy and politics. A natural roommate for David Batty, I thought immediately.'

803. 'We talked Alf Ramsey into letting us have a bit of sun by the hotel pool. He blew a whistle and we all lay down. Ten minutes later he blew it again and we all turned over.'

804. 'Of course I didn't take my wife to see Rochdale as an anniversary present. It was her birthday. Would I have got married in the football season? Anyway, it wasn't Rochdale, it was Rochdale Reserves.'

805. 'I'm called Trigger after Fools and Horses because I'm thick. It started at Liverpool in a pizza place. The waitress asked if I wanted my pizza cut into four pieces or eight. I chose four because there was no way I could eat eight.'

806. 'I used to love playing against English teams. They always gave you the ball back if you lost it. Still do.'

807. 'I hear Glenn Hoddle has found God. That must have been one hell of a pass.'

808. 'I met a man I'd lost track of and told him I was Millwall's player-manager. "How embarrassing," his wife replied immediately.'

809. 'Mind you, I've been here during the bad times too. One year we came second.'

810. 'There really is no upside to being caught dogging.'

Jasper Carrott
Jack Charlton
Stan Collymore
Johan Cruyff
Jason McAteer

Mick McCarthy
Bob Paisley
David Platt
Bill Shankly
Howard Wilkinson

QUOTES PART 2   82

Can you match the quotes with the names at the bottom of the page?

811. 'As we went out on the pitch, Tommy Smith handed me a piece of paper. It was the evening menu for the Liverpool Royal Infirmary.'

812. 'Even when they had Moore, Hurst and Peters, West Ham's average finish was about 17th. It just shows how crap the other eight of us were.'

813. 'A medal from Princess Di and a kiss from Sam Hammam, and with no disrespect to either, you wish it could have been the other way round.'

814. 'There'll be no siestas in Madrid tonight.'

815. 'Seaman, like a falling oak, manages to change direction.'

816. 'I never comment on referees, and I'm not going to break the habit of a lifetime for that prat.'

817. 'Our talking point this morning is George Best, his liver transplant and the booze culture in football. Don't forget, the best caller wins a crate of John Smith's.'

818. 'Becks hasn't changed since I've known him. He's always been a flash cockney git.'

819. 'Did I tell you Sinatra once met me?'

820. 'You can't say a word to them. It's not just Man United, but the modern player. They are not just weak players but are very weak human beings. They are quick to hide behind social media, their cars and their girlfriend's dog.'

Ron Atkinson
Alan Brazil
Brian Clough
Ryan Giggs
Jimmy Greaves

Vinnie Jones
Roy Keane
Kevin Keegan
John Motson
Harry Redknapp

83

REFEREES

821. Which Swedish referee quit the game in 2005 when Jose Mourinho questioned his integrity after a Barcelona v Chelsea Champions League game?

822. Which Englishman was in charge of the 1974 World Cup final between West Germany and Holland?

823. If you are my age you might know this one, otherwise you've got no chance! He was widely considered the best referee in the world because at that time it went without saying that England's best was also the world's best! He was in control of the 1952 FA Cup final between Newcastle United and Arsenal and later in life became a judge on TV's It's a Knockout. Who was he?

824. After refereeing the 2016 FA Cup final between Manchester United and Crystal Palace, he was tempted by the Saudis to become their new head of referees. Who is he?

825. Which Englishman who was in charge of the 2010 World Cupfinal ended up booking 13 players and sending one off in a game for which the Dutch had decided there was only one way to stop Spain?

826. Who was the referee in the Manchester United v Liverpool FA Cup final of 1996 who eventually took a job with Sky, analysing his fellow referees?

827. Which English referee in charge of of a 2006 World Cup match between Croatia and Australia mistakenly gave a Croatian three yellow cards before sending him off?

828. Why is Norwegian referee Tom Henning Øvrebø not over-popular down the Fulham Road?

829. What was unique about referee Alf Bond's being in control of the 1956 FA Cup final between Manchester City and Birmingham City?

830. He was the referee in the 1976 FA Cup final between Southampton and Manchester United but became known on the world stage when he blew for full-time in a 1978 World Cup game between Brazil and Sweden with the ball about to enter the Swedish net to give Brazil their winning goal. Who was he?

WORLD CUP - SCOTLAND 84
WALES, N IRELAND & ROI

831. Scotland's first World Cup was not a pleasant experience as they made an early exit after a 1-0 defeat by Austria and a 7-0 thrashing from a South American country that went on to beat England in the quarter-final. Who were they?

832. All four 'home' nations participated in the World Cup in Sweden in 1958. Which two reached the quarter-final after wins in play-offs?

833. The Republic of Ireland acquitted themselves well on their first visit to the World Cup, in Italy in 1990, beating Romania in a penalty shoot-out to reach the quarter-finals. Who scored the winning penalty?

834. Northern Ireland surprised their Spanish hosts in the 1982 World Cup by beating them 1-0 in their final group match. Who netted their winner?

835. Why did Scotland's qualification for the 1986 World Cup after a draw with Wales in September 1985 go largely uncelebrated?

836. In the 2002 World Cup Holland scored a goal but didn't play in the competition! Explain.

837. Which pair of brothers represented Wales in the 1958 World Cup in Sweden?

838. In that same 1958 World Cup, which Northern Ireland man, after scoring twice in the FA Cup final the previous year, did so again consecutively against both West Germany and Czechoslovakia?

839. In typical fashion, Scotland were terrible against both Peru and Iran in the 1978 World Cup in Argentina but, when things looked hopeless, turned in a great performance in their last game against Holland. Who scored a wonderful goal in that game and in which film does it appear?

840. Only one of those four nations took part in the 1998 competition in France. Which one was it?

85 SCOTTISH FOOTBALL

841. Which club won its only Scottish League title on goal average in 1964-65?

842. That 1964-65 season was unique in Scottish League history. Why?

843. Who are the most northerly club to win the Scottish FA Cup?

844. What was significant about the Rangers side that drew 0-0 with St Johnstone on 4 March 2000 at Ibrox Park?

845. Three fine centre halves – Ian Ure, Ron Yeats and Colin Hendry – all played their football in which city before their moves south of the border?

846. The very first season of the Scottish Championship of 1890-91 was the only one in which two teams on the same points total shared the title between them. Which two clubs were involved?

847. The name of the ground that this Scottish club played on from 1894 to 2009 was also the title of a song on Waiting for the Sun, the third album by The Doors. Who are the club and what was their ground called?

848. In the last nearly 50 years since the Scottish First Division fell by the wayside, the organisers have had three names for the top league in the country. These have been the Premier Division, the Premier League and the Premiership. However, whatever they call it, only two clubs in this period have broken the 'Old Firm' duopoly by winning it. Who are they?

849. Aberdeen, Celtic, Queen's Park, Rangers and Vale of Leven have all won the Scottish FA Cup three times in a row. Which one of those five has won it four times in succession?

850. Kris Boyd twice scored five goals in the Scottish League, first for Kilmarnock in 2004 and then for Rangers in 2009. They came against the same opposition. Who were they?

SENT OFF
PART 1   86

851. On 2 April 2005, Lee Bowyer and Kieron Dyer of Newcastle United were sent off for fighting each other when the home side went down 3-0 to which visitors?

852. Who, in 1985, was the first player to be sent off in an FA Cup final?

853. Who is the only man to be sent off at Wembley for both club and country?

854. Dennis Wise and Vinnie Jones were sent off the same number of times in their careers. How many times did they each see red, and for which two clubs were they both playing when they were sent off?

855. Who is the only goalkeeper to be sent off playing for England, receiving his marching orders in a World Cup qualifier against Ukraine in 2009?

856. Who, in the Aston Villa v Manchester United game in 1994, was the first player to be dismissed in a League Cup final?

857. On the first day of February 1995, Blackburn Rovers had goalkeeper Tim Flowers sent off after 72 seconds at Ewood Park. The point they extracted in a 1-1 draw after a colossal performance up front on his own from Alan Shearer was crucial at the season's end because without it there would have been no Premier League title. Who were they playing that night?

858. Which three Alans have been sent off playing for England?

859. Six players have been sent off in an FA Cup final, the most recent two for the same club. What is that club and who are the two players?

860. One player has been sent off while playing for five Premier League clubs. The clubs were Sheffield Wednesday, Leeds United, Southampton, Nottingham Forest and Coventry City. Who was the player?

89

87 SENT OFF PART 2

861. Firstly, a Manchester City player was sent off in the FA Cup final in 2013, then, three years later, it was the red half of the city that evened things up by having one of theirs receive a red card in the FA Cup final. Who were the two players?

862. When Sheffield Wednesday visited Wolves on 14 August 2000, their goalkeeper stayed on the pitch for just 13 seconds. Who was he?

863. Which Argentinian created a significant drama that went on for some time when the referee dismissed him in their quarter-final with England at Wembley in the 1966 World Cup?

864. Two London clubs had players with surnames starting with the same letter sent off in the Championship play-off finals of 2016 and 2018, against Derby County and Aston Villa. Who were the clubs and players?

865. I can't get worked up about the Charity Shield, but in 2000 a Manchester United player clearly did against Chelsea when he saw red in more ways than one. Who was he?

866. For a short spell Arsenal played Champions League football at Wembley, and in November 1998 had a player sent off at that venue against Lens. Who was he?

867. The first time four players were sent off in a Scottish game was in a Celtic v Rangers Scottish Cup quarter-final in 1991. Peter Grant was the lone hooped player and the three Rangers men were all English! Who were they?

868. Walter Boyd of Swansea City did something on 23 November 1999 at home to Darlington that can be equalled but not beaten. What was it?

869. Which Spurs defender saw a red card in the 92nd minute of their 3-1 win over Borussia Dortmund in September 2017?

870. Who might have been seen as a menace by opponents after seeing red 12 times in a career that took in Birmingham City, Southampton and QPR?

SIX OF THE BEST!   88

871. Which Yorkshire side are the only club to score six goals in an English League game and still lose?
A. Barnsley B. Huddersfield Town C. Leeds United D. York City

872. Against which clubs did both George Best for Manchester United and Denis Law for Manchester City score six away goals in FA Cup ties, in the latter case to no avail as the match was abandoned and City eventually lost?

873. Which English city's two teams have both played in six FA Cup finals?

874. Which are the only two countries to score six times against England in a match on English soil?

875. On 21 April 1930, an English League game ended in a 6-6 draw, a unique situation. The match took place at Filbert Street. Who were Leicester City's London-based visitors that day?

876. Which is the only country that has had its clubs win six successive European Cup finals, and which three clubs were involved?

877. Which six post-Second World War British Leeds United managers have taken charge of a club in a European final?

878. Who were the first six post-Second World War England goalkeepers to reach 50 caps for their country?

879. Who are the only club to have exactly six Football League titles to their name?

880. Which club finished as runners-up in the Third Division South six years in a row between 1921 and 1927, at a time when just one team were promoted from that division?

89 SUPPORTERS' SONGS

881. The Marcels, an American vocal group, had a No 1 hit in 1961 with a song that's become part of a particular club's tradition. Who are the club and what is the song?

882. Liverpool have possibly the most iconic football song with You'll Never Walk Alone. It came from a 1950s American musical via a recording by a Merseyside group. What were those two sources?

883. Tom Jones had a big hit in 1968 that was adopted as a club song. What song was it and whose supporters have sung it from that time on?

884. When Spurs won the title in 1951 their fans were singing an Irish song, but when the club won it again a decade later they were singing a song from the American Civil War they had adapted. What were the two songs?

885. Which Harry Lauder song from the 1920s has become Birmingham City's theme song?

886. The Huddie Ledbetter song Goodnight Irene from 1933 was used by supporters of which club after a version of it by The Weavers became popular in the 1950s?

887. A famous traditional jazz anthem from the early years of the 20th century became a very appropriate song for supporters of a particular southern club. Who are they and what song do their supporters sing?

888. The oldest song of all these, written in 1862, was originally about a northern sporting event and has been plagiarised by numerous clubs. What song is it and to which club does it belong?

889. A song written at the end of the First World War was popular in the early 1920s, when this club played in their first FA Cup final. Who were they and what was the song?

890. Written by William Ward-Higgs in 1907, this song is still heard when the teams come out for Brighton & Hove Albion's home games. What is it?

TEN PLAYERS, PLEASE!   90

... as we used to say upon entering the tobacconist's such a long time ago.

891. Who is the only player to score a hat-trick in all four divisions of the English League, the FA Cup, the League Cup and an international fixture?

892. Who is the only post-Second World War player to have captained a team to win both English and Scottish FA Cups?

893. Which foreign striker has registered hat-tricks for Portsmouth, Middlesbrough and Blackburn Rovers in the Premier League?

894. Before Riyad Mahrez equalled the feat in 2023, the only player to score a hat-trick in an FA Cup semi-final since the Second World War did so for Manchester United in a 5-3 replay win over Fulham at Highbury in 1958. Who was he?

895. Who is the only man to play in a Glasgow, a Manchester and a Merseyside derby?

896. Who is the only player to appear in a north London, a Manchester, a Merseyside and a Tyne-Wear derby?

897. Which two captains of English clubs were presented with major trophies in 1964, 1965 and 1966?

898. A player in the Spurs side that were the first to do the 'double' in the 20th century, in 1960-61, shares a surname with a member of the Arsenal team that in 2001-02 became the first to do so in the current century. Who were the two players?

899. Who is the only player since the Second World War to be capped for England while with a Welsh club?

900. If you were asked to name the best three midfield players in Spurs' history, Dave Mackay, Ossie Ardiles and Glenn Hoddle would figure in your thoughts. What is the link between them?

91 TRANSFER TRAIL

901. Mo Salah of Liverpool, Erik Lamela of Spurs and Antonio Rüdiger of Chelsea all came to the Premier League from the same club. Which one?

902. Which of the following four players is the odd one out and why? Marouane Fellaini, Tim Howard, Phil Neville and Morgan Schneiderlin.

903. Which centre forward joined Manchester United from Barnsley for £29,999 in 1952 so he wouldn't have the weight of being the first £30,000 player on his shoulders?

904. The only man to score more than 100 goals in both the English and Italian leagues moved from Charlton Athletic to Sampdoria in the mid-1950s. Who was he?

905. In the 1960s, Denis Law left Manchester City for a record fee to play in Italy. A year later he was back in Manchester, at United, after another record transfer. Which club did he play for during his Italian sojourn?

906. Chelsea bought David Luiz in 2011 for over £21 million, sold him in 2014 for £50 million and then bought him back for £32 million in 2016. I don't ask you to explain the apparently schizophrenic behaviour, merely to name the two other clubs involved in the transfers.

907. Which three Spanish clubs did the following three players come from? Diego Costa of Chelsea, Eric Bailly of Manchester United and David Silva of Manchester City.

908. Who was Bournemouth's first £20 million player in June 2017?

909. Which player moved from São Paulo to PSG in 2013 before joining Spurs in 2018?

910. Between 2014 and 2018, Southampton sold six players to Liverpool. How many can you name?

UEFA CUP 1972-2009   92

911. Which player scored for Stuttgart in the 1989 UEFA Cup final and again for Bayern Munich in 1996, and in between made a few friends at White Hart Lane?

912. Which two players with the same surname scored two goals each over the two legs of the 1993 final to give Juventus victory over Borussia Dortmund?

913. Which two clubs have won consecutive UEFA Cups, the first in 1985 and 1986 and the second in 2006 and 2007?

914. Which Italian side won the trophy three times in the 1990s?

915. In the penultimate final in 2008, which produced a win for Zenit St Petersburg over Glasgow Rangers, the venue was an English club ground. Which one?

916. Which Swedish club were twice successful in the competition in the 1980s?

917. Which German club appeared in four finals in the first nine years of the competition, winning two and losing two, but never got that far again in the last 29 years it ran for?

918. Considering English clubs' success in the competition, Bill Nicholson, Bill Shankly and Bob Paisley were the first three managers to lift the cup. Who was the fourth?

919. The 2001 final between Liverpool and Alavés ended with the rarity of a 'golden own goal' that gave Liverpool a memorable 5-4 win. Who came off the subs' bench to put them 4-3 up, who equalised for Alavés in the 89th minute, and how many players were on the pitch when the game ended?

920. The curtain came down on the competition in 2009 with Shakhtar Donetsk beating Werder Bremen. Which city became the last one to host a UEFA Cup final?
A – Istanbul B – Lisbon C – Moscow D – Paris

93

WHERE?

All these top players appeared for clubs with which you wouldn't normally associate them.

921. Bobby Smith and Martin Chivers, two of Spurs' top post-Second World War strikers, both ended up for a short spell at the end of their careers at which club?

922. Towards the end of their playing days, Paul Gascoigne and Ian Wright rocked up at the same place. Which club was it?

923. George Best's last club in the early 1980s didn't get much for their money as he played just five times for them. Who were they?

924. Besides West Ham United, Chelsea and Manchester City, which other British club has Frank Lampard played for?

925. Merseyside stars of the 1960s, Gordon West at Everton and Ron Yeats at Liverpool, both ended their careers at the same club not far away from their earlier heady days. Which club did they play for?

926. Alan Ball and Mick Channon between them made more than 700 appearances for Southampton. For which other club did they both play a few times?

927. Tony Currie was something of a legend at Sheffield United, but the last 14 games of his career took place with a club, significantly southwest of Yorkshire, that are currently not in the League. Who were they?

928. Manchester United's Gary Pallister, in his Middlesbrough days, went out on loan and played seven times at a club no longer playing in the League. Who were they?

929. Everton's great 'keeper Neville Southall ended his career with nine outings for which club?

930. Chelsea star John Terry spent six games on loan at which Midlands club in the year 2000?

WORLD CUP 1930-1978: COUNTRIES 94

931. Which two countries won the first two World Cups they entered?

932. In which year's World Cup was there no actual final, the winner being decided by the final pool league match?

933. West Germany won the 1954 World Cup in Switzerland by beating Hungary 3-2 in the final after being 2-0 down. The two countries had met each other earlier in the tournament. How had that game turned out?

934. In the first seven World Cups between 1930 and 1962, two nations reached the final twice but failed to win it. Who were they?

935. In the 1966 event that was held in England, one of the four quarter-finals produced as many goals as the other three put together. The two teams produced an eight-goal thriller. Who were they and what was the score?

936. In the first World Cup in 1930, which two countries reached the semi-final but have been unable to get that far again?

937. Which country in 1978 became the first to be runners-up in successive World Cup finals?

938. The third-place match is one of the most pointless things in existence, but in 1958 it produced a nine-goal bonanza between two European countries that ended 6-3. Which two countries provided the entertainment?

939. Which country appeared in the first and last World Cup final in this period?

940. Which was the only country to be World Cup winners three times in this period?

95 WORLD CUP 1930-1978: PLAYERS

941. Who scored in all six matches for Brazil in the 1970 World Cup in Mexico?

942. Who captained Argentina when they won the World Cup in 1978?

943. In the 1958 World Cup in Sweden, which Frenchman scored 13 goals in the tournament, a record that still stands?

944. What is Joe Gaetjens famous for?

945. Who scored for Brazil in both the 1958 and 1962 World Cup finals?

946. Who put the Dutch ahead from the penalty spot in the first minute of the 1974 final against West Germany? A. Johan Cruyff B. Johan Neeskens C. Rob Rensenbrink D. Johnny Rep

947. In 1930, Uruguay had a goalscorer in the final who shared his name with a political leader on the world stage a generation later, and a goalkeeper who shared his name with a golfer with five Majors to his name. What were the two players' surnames?

948. In which two years did the winners in the final have two players who each scored twice?

949. In this period both Pelé of Brazil and Uwe Seeler of West Germany appeared in four World Cup competitions, but one man went one better with five. Unsurprisingly, he was a goalkeeper. Who was he and which country did he represent?

950. While on the subject of goalkeepers, the two men that stood between the posts when Brazil won in 1970 and when Argentina were victorious in 1978 share the same first letter of their names. Who were they?

WORLD CUP 1982-2022: COUNTRIES   96

951. In the 2006 tournament in Germany, which nation reached the semi-final for the first time in 40 years?

952. Which country have played in two semi-finals in this period but have never reached the final in any period?

953. Which two countries who have never won the trophy or appeared in any other semi-final nevertheless both reached the semi-final stage at the 2002 World Cup competition?

954. Which country in the United States World Cup of 1994 became the most northerly before or since to reach the last four in this period?

955. Which two countries met each other in three World Cup finals in this period?

956. In these 11 World Cups how many ended with European wins?

957. Besides Brazil and Argentina, who are the only South American nation to get to a semi-final of the World Cup in this period?

958. Which country reached the semi-final stage twice in this period, in 1990 and 2018?

959. Which are the only two countries that have appeared in a World Cup final in this period but have never won the competition at any point in their histories?

960. A tough one to finish: who were the only nation in the 2010 World Cup in South Africa to go home undefeated?

97 WORLD CUP 1982-2022: PLAYERS

961. Which four men have scored more than once in a World Cup final in this period?

962. Who scored for both sides in the France v Croatia World Cup final of 2018?

963. During this period five players scored from the penalty spot in a World Cup final. The penalties were taken in 1990, 2006, 2018 and 2022 by which five players?

964. The 1982 semi-final between West Germany and France saw a violent challenge, in which the German goalkeeper put a French forward in hospital and ensured extra support for the Italians in the final against Germany, go unpunished. Which two players were involved?

965. Which four men who have played for Chelsea were in the French team that won the World Cup in 1998?

966. Italy's three goals in the 1982 final were scored by players whose names ended with the same letter. Who were the three?

967. Who, in scoring a hat-trick against Spain in 2018, became only the fourth player in history to score in four World Cup competitions?

968. Who, in that 2018 World Cup, was named the Player of the Tournament?

969. When England beat Argentina 1-0 in a 2002 group game, the win was achieved with a David Beckham penalty for a foul on Michael Owen. The man who gave away the penalty became better known in England over a decade later. Who was he?

970. Only one surname has appeared twice among winners of the 'Golden Boot' in World Cup history. It happened in the earlier period, in 1970, and then again in this period when the Golden Boot was shared four ways in 2010. Who were the two men with the same surname?

YOU'RE HIRED!   98

971. Starting in the late 1970s, which club hired three ex-Leeds United players in a row as manager, and then gave the first of them a second go at the job? The players were Allan Clarke, Norman Hunter and Bobby Collins.

972. Who is the only man to be hired three times as manager of Everton?

973. In the 1990s Spurs hired three managers in a row whose surnames ended in the same letter. Who were the three?

974. Which club hired just four managers in the first 72 years of its existence, but in this century has given someone the job, sacked him and then rehired him?

975. In the first decade of this century, Fulham employed five managers in succession who either had been or eventually became managers of a national team. Who were they? PS: Kevin Keegan isn't one of them as he left in 1999.

976. Frank McLintock captained Arsenal to the FA Cup in 1971 and ten years later Steve Perryman did the same for Spurs. They followed each other in that order as managers of which club in the 1980s?

977. Between 1965 and 1989 Birmingham City hired four managers who had won the Football League with other clubs. Who were they?

978. Nine Chelsea managers scored a goal in an FA Cup final in their playing careers. How many can you name?

979. Peterborough United were managed consecutively in the 1950s by Jack Fairbrother and George Swindin. What else linked them?

980. Sam Allardyce has been hired as the manager of four Lancastrian town clubs, one of them as caretaker-manager. Who are the four?

99 YOU'RE FIRED!

981. It was supposed to be a whole new approach to the game, but it took Crystal Palace just four games at the start of the 2017-18 season to decide it wasn't for them after all. Who bit the dust?

982. Paul Gascoigne lasted just 39 days before being sacked as manager of which non-League club in December 2005?

983. Which man, who as a player missed just two League games for Blackburn Rovers when they took the Premier League title in 1994-95, lasted just 57 days as the club's manager before his dismissal in December 2012?

984. Tommy Docherty in 1968 and Paul Hart in 2010 both lasted exactly 28 days as manager of which club?

985. In October 1981 Leyton Orient fired their manager after he had been in the job for just 20 days. He had the perfect name for a sacked manager. What was it?

986. Two great managers both lasted just 44 days at Leeds United, the first in 1974 and the second in 1978. Who were they?

987. The shortest residency of management for a British nation is 48 days. Which Welshman lasted this long before his sacking in March 1994, but did return to the job in the following century?

988. Playing nearly 400 times for Norwich City did not give this man much leeway when the club called time on his managerial career just six days into the 2009-10 season. Who was he?

989. Thirty years after the greatest day in his life, which manager was moved on by Manchester City within 12 days of the start of the 1996-97 season?

990. Mark Hughes has the unenviable record of being the first manager to be sacked by two Premier League clubs in the same calendar year. Which two clubs decided he wasn't for them in 2018?

'Z'

100

Almost at the end of the quiz, we come to the last letter of the alphabet. Everyone likes a 'Z' except perhaps Bob Dylan, who threw his away! So here goes ...

991. Who became the first man to win the World Cup as a player and as a manager when Brazil won the competition in 1970?
992. Which classy German international scored for Spurs against Blackburn Rovers in the 2002 League Cup final?
993. Which player who appeared, amongst others, for Liverpool and Chelsea, scored from the penalty spot for Middlesbrough against Bolton Wanderers the 2004 League Cup final, although it looked like he had kicked the ball twice?
994. Which Brazilian won two World Cup winners' medals, in 1958 and 1962, scoring one of the goals in the latter win?
995. This man, with the exception of a short spell in Manchester that didn't work out, has strutted his stuff down the wing at Selhurst Park for over a decade. Who is he?
996. Which player with a surname beginning with 'Z' has appeared in consecutive FA Cup finals for Chelsea in this century?
997. Which legendary goalkeeper captained Italy to their 1982 World Cup success?
998. The 2017 FA Cup final between Arsenal and Chelsea was notable for containing in the two clubs' squads seven players with a 'z' in their names. Five started the match and the other two, one from each side, were unused substitutes. How many can you name?
999. The 1915 FA Cup final between Sheffield United and Chelsea was the first occasion when a goal was scored by a player with a 'z' in his name. That surname was shared over half a century later by the man who still holds Blackburn Rovers' appearances record. What was that surname?
1000. Arguably Chelsea's most popular player, he scored the goal that won the European Cup Winners' Cup final in 1998, and the way he played the game makes him the perfect end to this marathon. Who was he?

BONUS: THE QATAR WORLD CUP 2022

The awarding of the 2022 World Cup to Qatar by FIFA in 2010 was controversial to say the least. Among all the other issues and allegations of corruption, I found it absurd that a country devoid of any football history and without a single league could be given a World Cup. Also, their original bid was for the normal summer time for the competition.

It was incredible that not one of the thousands involved in the issue put up their hand just once to ask whether it was physically impossible to play in the intense heat of Qatar at that time of year. Because of FIFA's support of the bid despite this nonsensical situation, all established football leagues throughout the world were forced to uproot their programmes and threaten the careers of players by making them play three times a week for five months after a draining World Cup. Madness reigns! I wonder why?

1. Which two countries from the same qualifying group reached the Qatar World Cup despite both of them losing six matches at the qualifying stage?

2. Who were the only country that World Cup winners Argentina lost to during the competition?

3. Kylian Mbappé and Lionel Messi dominated the tournament, the Frenchman taking the Golden Boot and equalling Geoff Hurst's record of a World Cup final hat-trick, while the Argentinian got his much-deserved World Cup winner's medal at last and was the Player of the Tournament. How many goals did they score between them?

4. Which two players, one from each of those teams, shared third place in the scoring stakes with four apiece?

5. Concerning World Cup goalscorers with Manchester United connections, the number nearly reached double figures. Two of them had surnames starting with D. Who were they?

6. There were five instances of games being decided by penalty shoot-outs. Which two countries were successful more than once by this method?

7. Who were the only one of the eight countries involved in a penalty shoot-out to miss all their penalties?

THE QATAR WORLD CUP 2022 — BONUS

8. Which nation, who were ranked second in the world before the competition, failed to get out of Group F?
9. Which country were the only one that England failed to score against?
10. Which Netherlands player found the net in all three group matches?
11. Which Spanish city scored the tournament's first two goals when Ecuador beat the hosts?
12. The only hat-trick in 90 minutes in the competition came from Gonçalo Ramos, who shared that surname with the referee! Which nation won 6-1 on 6 December to reach the quarter-final stage, and which nation went home?
13. Which two players scored twice when England met Iran on 21 November, running out 6-2 winners?
14. The biggest margin of victory in the tournament came via a 7-0 scoreline in Group E on 23 November. Which two nations contested the game?
15. USA v Iran is always a powder-keg encounter. The Americans shaded this one through the game's only goal. Who scored it and which club does he play for?
16. No nation left the tournament without scoring at least once. True or false?
17. Which country must have gone home ecstatic after landing the Fair Play award?
18. How did Alireza Beiranvand and Hossein Hosseini make history at this World Cup?
19. Add the number of matches in this World Cup to the number of teams in the inclusivity-mad 2026 edition. What number do you end up with?
20. The Third Place match is an entirely pointless affair that nobody wants to see, let alone play in! Which two nations contested it this time around? It does have a purpose after all — I've used it to finish the quiz!

REAL FOOTY FANS QUIZ BOOK ANSWERS

QUIZ NO 1 - ANYTHING GOES PART 1
1. Carling, Carabao, Coca-Cola, Milk and Worthington.
2. Leeds United in 1992-93.
3. France (in Paris each time).
4. Joe Fagan.
5. Germany – Munich 1974 and Berlin 2006.
6. Manchester City.
7. Turkey.
8. Chelsea.
9. Alan Smith – Leeds United, Newcastle United and Manchester United.
10. Torino.

QUIZ NO 2 - ANYTHING GOES PART 2
11. Birmingham City.
12. St Etienne.
13. Lee Martin – against Crystal Palace in 1990. The actor was Lee Marvin.
14. They were all England captains on the night in 2003 when England met Montenegro at Leicester, due to Eriksson's pointless substitutions.
15. Dundee.
16. John Ruddy and Declan Rudd.
17. Holdsworth.
18. John Barnes, Kenny Dalglish – 'Super Caley go ballistic, Celtic are atrocious'.
19. Michael Laudrup.
20. They were the clubs at the top of the four divisions when the 1939-40 season was aborted after three games.

QUIZ NO 3 - APPEARANCES (CAN BE DECEPTIVE!)
21. Dave Beasant.
22. Alan Ball.
23. John Hollins.
24. Leicester City, Stoke City, Nottingham Forest, Southampton and Derby County.
25. Birmingham City.
26. Brentford.
27. Pat Jennings and David James.
28. Ernie Moss.
29. He played 344 times for each club.
30. John Trollope.

QUIZ NO 4 - 'BOYS OF '66'
31. Nobby Stiles and Bobby Charlton.
32. George Cohen.
33. Roger Hunt.
34. Gordon Banks.
35. Martin Peters.
36. Jack Charlton.
37. Bobby Moore.
38. Geoff Hurst – Stoke City and WBA.
39. Alan Ball.

40. Ray Wilson.

QUIZ NO 5 - BRITISH CLUBS IN EUROPE PART 1

41. Arsenal – 1994 and 1995.
42. Leeds United – 1968 and 1971.
43. Glasgow Rangers in 1972 and Manchester United in 1999.
44. Rotterdam.
45. Nottingham Forest, Spurs and West Ham United.
46. Birmingham City.
47. Anderlecht.
48. Hibernian.
49. Bayern Munich.
50. C – Swansea City.

QUIZ NO 6 - BRITISH CLUBS IN EUROPE PART 2

51. Liverpool – against Real Madrid.
52. Diego Forlan.
53. Mark Hughes and Ronald Koeman – both managed Southampton.
54. Rafael Benítez.
55. Celtic.
56. The goal was scored by ex-Spur Nayim.
57. Dundee United.
58. Arsenal – to Valencia and Galatasaray.
59. Pat Holland, Mike England and Alan Brazil.
60. Hampden Park, Glasgow.

QUIZ NO 7 - BROTHERS

61. Bobby and Jack Charlton.
62. Ron and Allan Harris.
63. Rafael and Fábio Da Silva.
64. Denis and Leslie Compton.
65. Jimmy and Brian Greenhoff.
66. Danny, Rodney and Ray Wallace.
67. Gary and Phil Neville.
68. George and Ted Robledo.
69. Kolo and Yaya Touré.
70. Kenny and Terry Hibbitt.

QUIZ NO 8 - CHAMPIONS LEAGUE 1993-2023 - CLUBS

71. FC Porto and Monaco.
72. Real Madrid – in Glasgow and Cardiff.
73. Juventus and Valencia.
74. Arsenal, Liverpool, Chelsea and Manchester United.
75. Bayern Munich.
76. Marseille.
77. AC Milan.
78. Bayern Munich and Borussia Dortmund.
79. Barcelona.
80. Arsenal, Chelsea and Spurs.

QUIZ NO 9 - CHAMPIONS LEAGUE 1993-2023 - PLAYERS

81. Peter Schmeichel.
82. Steve McManaman.
83. Hernán Crespo.
84. Sol Campbell.
85. Filippo Inzaghi.
86. Didier Drogba.
87. Arjen Robben.
88. Sergio Ramos.
89. Paul Lambert.
90. Clarence Seedorf.

QUIZ NO 10 - CRICKETING FOOTBALLERS

91. Ken Grieves.
92. Chris Balderstone.
93. Denis Compton.
94. Jim Standen.
95. Jack Dyson.
96. Jim Cumbes.
97. Ken Taylor.
98. Arthur Milton.
99. Willie Watson.
100. Brian Close.

QUIZ NO 11 - CRYPTIC CLUBS

101. Stoke.
102. Hearts.
103. Reading.
104. Oldham.
105. Clyde.
106. Crystal Palace.
107. Hamilton.
108. Albion Rovers.
109. Southend.
110. Motherwell.

QUIZ NO 12 - CRYPTIC FA CUP FINAL GOALSCORERS

111. Alan Sunderland.
112. Raheem Sterling.
113. Jack Stamps.
114. Garth Crooks.
115. Teddy Sheringham.
116. Jack and Terry Dyson.
117. John Anderson.
118. Roy Dwight.
119. Reg Lewis, Ben Watson and Jimmy Case.
120. Ian St John, Frank Saul and Gabriel Jesus (the latter has two!).

QUIZ NO 13 - CRYPTIC MANAGERS

121. Ian Holloway.
122. Kenny Jackett.
123. Roberto Mancini.
124. Joe Jordan.
125. Dave Sexton.
126. Christian Gross.
127. Matt Busby.
128. Danny Wilson and Adrian Heath.
129. Russell Slade.
130. Sunderland - with Alan Durban, Mick Buxton, Ken Knighton, Malcolm Crosby, Tom Watson and Howard Wilkinson.

QUIZ NO 14 - ENGLAND GOALKEEPERS

131. Ray Wood and Chris Woods.
132. Ben Foster and Fraser Forster.
133. Gordon Banks and Jack Butland.
134. Gil Merrick.
135. Peter Shilton and David James.
136. Luton Town.
137. Paul Robinson.
138. Frank Swift.
139. Scott Carson.
140. David Seaman and Joe Hart.

QUIZ NO 15 - ENGLAND GOALSCORERS

141. David Platt and Ian Wright.
142. 30.
143. Theo Walcott.

144. Nick Barmby.
145. Wayne Rooney.
146. Bryan Robson.
147. Matthew Upson.
148. A scoring rate above a goal a game.
149. Geoff Hurst and Martin Peters.
150. Bobby Charlton.

QUIZ NO 16 - ENGLAND MANAGERS

151. Gareth Southgate - with Aston Villa in 2000.
152. Terry Venables and Roy Hodgson - the latter was in charge of Switzerland.
153. Sam Allardyce - one game, one win!
154. Walter Winterbottom.
155. Alf Ramsey.
156. Graham Taylor and Glenn Hoddle.
157. Alf Ramsey, Don Revie, Joe Mercer and Howard Wilkinson.
158. Steve McClaren.
159. Bobby Robson, Sven-Göran Eriksson and Fabio Capello.
160. Joe Mercer, Kevin Keegan, Sven-Göran Eriksson and Stuart Pearce.

QUIZ NO 17 - ENGLAND V GERMANY

161. England, Spain, Mexico, Italy, South Africa.
162. Charleroi and Alan Shearer.
163. Nobby Stiles.
164. Uwe Seeler.
165. Stanley Matthews.
166. D - White Hart Lane.
167. Özil, Mertesacker and Podolski.
168. Roger Byrne, Duncan Edwards and Tommy Taylor.
169. B - Detroit.
170. Didi Hamann and Owen Hargreaves.

QUIZ NO 18 - ENGLAND IN THE WORLD CUP 1950-1982

171. 1974 and 1978.
172. Billy Wright.
173. Brazil.
174. Switzerland.
175. Alan Ball, Geoff Hurst and Martin Peters.
176. Trevor Francis.
177. Ron Flowers.
178. Bryan Robson - v France in 1982.
179. Mick Mills and Paul Mariner.
180. Gerry Hitchens - Inter Milan.

QUIZ NO 19 - ENGLAND IN THE WORLD CUP 1986-2022

181. David Beckham, Harry Kane, Gary Lineker and Alan Shearer.
182. Morocco.
183. Mark Wright.
184. Harry Maguire, John Stones and Kieran Trippier.
185. Costa Rica.
186. Cameroon.
187. C - Paraguay.
188. Rob Green and Clint Dempsey.
189. Steven Gerrard.
190. Tunisia, Colombia and Romania.

QUIZ NO 20 – EUROPA LEAGUE 2010-2023

191. Manchester United.
192. Marseille.
193. Benfica.
194. Villareal.
195. André Villas-Boas.
196. Inter Milan.
197. Simon Davies.
198. Germany.
199. Chelsea, Arsenal and Baku.
200. Paul Pogba, Henrikh Mkhitaryan and Edinson Cavani.

QUIZ NO 21 – EUROPEAN CUP 1956-1992 – CLUBS

201. Red Star Belgrade.
202. Reims.
203. Munich and Madrid.
204. Barcelona.
205. Ajax and Bayern Munich.
206. AS Roma.
207. Real Madrid and Inter Milan.
208. Liverpool.
209. 1974.
210. Inter Milan and Benfica.

QUIZ NO 22 – EUROPEAN CUP 1956-1992 – PLAYERS

211. Alfredo di Stéfano.
212. Billy McNeill of Celtic.
213. Nigel Spink.
214. Michel Platini.
215. Tommy Gemmell.
216. Ferenc Puskás.
217. Ruud Gullit and Marco van Basten.
218. Bobby Charlton.
219. Phil Neal.
220. C – Israel.

QUIZ NO 23 – EUROPEAN CUP WINNERS' CUP 1961-1999

221. Fiorentina and Lazio.
222. C – Rotterdam.
223. Aberdeen, Arsenal, Chelsea, Everton, Manchester City, Manchester United, Rangers, Spurs and West Ham United – Chelsea won it twice.
224. B – Jones.
225. Peter Osgood.
226. Anderlecht.
227. Luca Vialli.
228. Ronaldo.
229. Smith – Arsenal, Liverpool, Rangers and Spurs.
230. He was the only player to score two twice in the final.

QUIZ NO 24 – EUROS 1960-2020 – COUNTRIES

231. Portugal.
232. Spain.
233. West Germany.
234. The Soviet Union.
235. Yugoslavia.
236. Holland, the Soviet Union and the Republic of Ireland.
237. France.
238. Greece and Portugal.
239. Iceland and Italy.
240. Denmark – it was extra special because Sweden were the hosts.

QUIZ NO 25 - EUROS 1960-2020 - PLAYERS

241. Frank Lampard.
242. Fernando Torres.
243. Gareth Bale.
244. Zinedine Zidane.
245. Patrik Berger.
246. Jean Tigana.
247. Luke Shaw.
248. David Trezeguet.
249. Iker Casillas and Gianluigi Buffon.
250. Gerd Müller.

QUIZ NO 26 - FA CUP 1872-1939 - CLUBS

251. The Wanderers.
252. Aston Villa and WBA.
253. Blackburn Rovers.
254. Huddersfield Town and Preston North End.
255. Bury.
256. Barnsley.
257. Manchester City and Bradford City.
258. B – Old Etonians.
259. Arsenal.
260. C – Bolton Wanderers.

QUIZ NO 27 - FA CUP 1872-1939 - PLAYERS

261. Dick Pym.
262. David Jack.
263. Steve Bloomer.
264. He captained Cardiff City, the first non-English winners.
265. Brown, Smith and Cameron.
266. Stan Seymour.
267. CB Fry.
268. Newcastle United and Wolves.
269. Harold Halse.
270. Jack Roscamp.

QUIZ NO 28 - FA CUP 1946-1999 - CLUBS

271. Leicester City.
272. Arsenal, Everton and Manchester United.
273. Blackpool.
274. Coventry City and Wimbledon.
275. Charlton Athletic.
276. Manchester United.
277. Liverpool and Newcastle United.
278. Fulham and Ipswich Town.
279. Southampton.
280. Whoever won these FA Cup finals, a new name would have been engraved on the Cup.

QUIZ NO 29 - FA CUP 1946-1999 - PLAYERS

281. Kenny Dalglish.
282. John Barnes – for Watford, Liverpool and Newcastle United.
283. Eric Cantona.
284. Paul Bracewell.
285. Bill Slater.
286. Howard Kendall.
287. Johnny Giles.
288. Stan Mortensen.
289. Bobby Moore.
290. George Hannah.

QUIZ NO 30 - FA CUP 2000-2022 - CLUBS

291. Chelsea.
292. Wigan Athletic.
293. Arsenal.
294. Liverpool.
295. Aston Villa.
296. Stoke City.
297. West Ham United.
298. Hull City - the other club was Arsenal.
299. Blackburn Rovers, Newcastle United and Spurs.
300. Arsenal and Chelsea.

QUIZ NO 31 - FA CUP 2000-2022 - PLAYERS

301. Dennis Wise and Tim Cahill.
302. Didier Drogba.
303. Fredrik Ljungberg.
304. Louis Saha.
305. Gabriel Jesus and Raheem Sterling.
306. Frank Lampard and Kevin-Prince Boateng.
307. Paul Scholes.
308. Paul Jones.
309. Ruud van Nistelrooy, Eden Hazard and Pierre-Emerick Aubameyang.
310. Matthew Etherington.

QUIZ NO 32 - FA CUP CURIOSITIES PART 1

311. Manchester United entered a FIFA event and did not defend the FA Cup. Money talks, as JJ Cale once said! This left an odd number of clubs. Previous losers drew lots to see who would get a second chance. Darlington won.
312. Adrian Heath and Nigel Callaghan.
313. Flanagan and Allen.
314. James Dean - Alex James and Dixie Dean.
315. Batty - Ron and David.
316. Trevor Cherry and David Peach.
317. Nicky Holmes (Southampton), Dave Watson (Sunderland) and Alan Hudson (Arsenal).
318. Byrne - Manchester United, West Ham United, Liverpool and Sunderland.
319. Price - David for Arsenal, Paul for Spurs and Neil for Watford.
320. Joe Bradford.

QUIZ NO 33 - FA CUP CURIOSITIES PART 2

321. Jeff Hall and Ken Green - Hall Green Stadium, Birmingham.
322. Geoff Pike.
323. Marc Overmars.
324. Aston Villa - John Aston and Ricardo Villa.
325. Jimmy Nelson.
326. Valencia.
327. Alan Ball.
328. Chester.
329. Dave Beasant, David Seaman and Kasper Schmeichel.
330. Manchester - Fallowfield and Old Trafford.

QUIZ NO 34 - FA CUP GIANTKILLERS

331. Harry Redknapp.
332. Birmingham City.
333. Yeovil Town.
334. Worcester City.
335. Walsall.
336. Colchester United.
337. Chelsea and Sunderland.
338. Hereford United, Wimbledon, Sutton United and Histon.
339. Aston Villa.
340. Luton Town and Norwich City.

QUIZ NO 35 - FAIRS CUP 1958-1971

341. B – Barcelona.
342. Leeds United.
343. Birmingham City.
344. Arsenal.
345. D – Roma.
346. Newcastle United.
347. D – Valencia.
348. Ferencváros.
349. B – Stamford Bridge.
350. Jimmy Greaves and Allan Clarke.

QUIZ NO 36 - FATHERS AND SONS

351. Peter and Kasper Schmeichel.
352. Steve and Alex Bruce.
353. Frank Lampard – Senior and Junior.
354. John Aston – Senior and Junior.
355. Brian and Nigel Clough.
356. Ian Wright and Shaun Wright-Phillips.
357. Harry and Jamie Redknapp.
358. Iceland.
359. Kelly.
360. Herd.

QUIZ NO 37 - FOOTBALL AROUND THE COUNTRY: LANCASHIRE

361. Rochdale.
362. Preston North End.
363. Blackpool and Bolton Wanderers.
364. Stockport County.
365. Wigan Athletic.
366. Burnley.
367. Manchester City.
368. Oldham Athletic and Bolton Wanderers.
369. Bury.
370. Blackburn Rovers and Accrington.

QUIZ NO 38 - FOOTBALL AROUND THE COUNTRY: LONDON

371. Brentford.
372. Arsenal.
373. West Ham United.
374. Millwall.
375. QPR.
376. Fulham.
377. Crystal Palace.
378. Wimbledon.
379. Leyton Orient.
380. Spurs at Stamford Bridge in 1921.

QUIZ NO 39 - FOOTBALL AROUND THE COUNTRY: THE MIDLANDS

381. Notts County in 1894 and Nottingham Forest in 1898.
382. Walsall.
383. WBA.
384. Trevor Francis moved from Birmingham City to Nottingham Forest.

385. Coventry City in 1987.
386. Derby County.
387. Derby County and Nottingham Forest – Brian Clough.
388. Wolves.
389. Leicester City and Stoke City.
390. Birmingham City, Coventry City, Notts County, Stoke City and Walsall.

QUIZ NO 40 – FOOTBALL AROUND THE COUNTRY: THE NORTH EAST

391. Bob Stokoe – Newcastle United in 1955, Sunderland in 1973.
392. Sunderland.
393. Stan Anderson.
394. Újpest Dózsa and Seville.
395. Middlesbrough, Sunderland and Hartlepools United.
396. Whitley Bay.
397. Bishop Auckland and Crook Town.
398. Darlington and Hartlepools United.
399. Gateshead.
400. Sam Allardyce, Kevin Keegan, Steve McClaren, Bobby Robson, Gareth Southgate and Terry Venables.

QUIZ NO 41 – FOOTBALL AROUND THE COUNTRY: SOUTH OF LONDON (EAST, WEST AND CENTRAL)

401. Exeter City.
402. Brighton.
403. Bournemouth.
404. Portsmouth.
405. Peter Taylor.
406. The Dell, Southampton.
407. Plymouth Argyle.
408. Won the FA Cup while managing Portsmouth.
409. Torquay United.
410. Bury and Sheffield United.

QUIZ NO 42 – FOOTBALL AROUND THE COUNTRY: YORKSHIRE

411. Rotherham United, Leeds United, Sheffield Wednesday and Bradford City.
412. Alan Hodgkinson, Ron Springett, Chris Woods, Nigel Martyn and Paul Robinson.
413. Doncaster Rovers.
414. Huddersfield Town (1923-24 to 1925-26), Leeds United (1969-70 to 1971-72) and Sheffield Wednesday (1930-31 to 1932-33).
415. Hull City and Sheffield United – 2014 – Hull won 5-3.
416. Bradford City and Barnsley.
417. Huddersfield Town.
418. Tony Currie and Mick Jones.
419. Bradford Park Avenue.
420. York City.

QUIZ NO 43 – FOOTBALLER OF THE YEAR

421. Chris Waddle.
422. Scott Parker.
423. Bobby Collins, Jack Charlton, Billy Bremner and Norman Hunter.
424. Jamie Vardy and Riyad Mahrez.
425. N'Golo Kanté.

426. Dennis Bergkamp, Robert Pires, Thierry Henry and Robin van Persie.
427. Bert Trautmann, Gordon Banks, Peter Shilton, Neville Southall and Pat Jennings.
428. Stanley Matthews, Gary Lineker, Kevin Keegan and Alan Shearer.
429. Roy Keane, Teddy Sheringham and Ruud van Nistelrooy.
430. Andy Gray, David Platt and Paul McGrath.

QUIZ NO 44 - FOOTBALL ODDITIES

431. The 32 matches produced no replays.
432. John Collins and Collins John.
433. Panathinaikos.
434. They had the best defensive record in the league.
435. Peters and Lee.
436. Pat Rice and Patrice Evra.
437. Manchester City.
438. Barnes Bridge – the players are John Barnes and Wayne Bridge.
439. Maine Road – Old Trafford was not ready due to war damage and United shared City's ground.
440. Darren and Marcus Bent.

QUIZ NO 45 - GLOBETROTTING GOALIES

441. Sander Westerveld.
442. Petr Čech.
443. Kasey Keller, Espen Baardsen and Brad Friedel.
444. David Ospina, Arsenal and Colombia.
445. Erik Thorstvedt and Frode Grodås.
446. Willy Caballero.
447. Jens Lehmann and Bernd Leno.
448. Luděk Mikloško.
449. Pepe Reina and Joel Robles.
450. Edwin van der Sar, Peter Enckelman and Tim Howard.

QUIZ NO 46 - GOALSCORING GOALIES

451. Paul Robinson (for Spurs and Leeds United).
452. Asmir Begović and Artur Boruc.
453. Jimmy Glass.
454. Mark Crossley.
455. Brad Friedel.
456. Pat Jennings.
457. Alex Stepney.
458. Peter Schmeichel.
459. Steve Sherwood and Steve Ogrizovic.
460. Ray Charles.

QUIZ NO 47 - GOALSCORING HEROES

461. Sadio Mané.
462. Peter Crouch.
463. Ole Gunnar Solskjaer.
464. Geoff Hurst – FA Cup, League Cup, European Cup Winners' Cup and World Cup.
465. Wayne Rooney.
466. Roger Hunt, Luis Suárez and Mo Salah.
467. Alan Shearer.
468. Thierry Henry.
469. Chelsea, AC Milan, Spurs and West Ham United.
470. Arthur Rowley.

QUIZ NO 48 - GROUNDS (BUILT POST-SECOND WORLD WAR)

471. The Reebok Stadium, Bolton - named after a pair of trainers!
472. The Stadium of Light, Sunderland.
473. The Sixfields Stadium, Northampton.
474. The New York Stadium, Rotherham United.
475. The St Mary's Stadium, Southampton.
476. Vale Park, Port Vale.
477. Adams Park, Wycombe Wanderers - the manager was Tony Adams.
478. The London Stadium, West Ham United.
479. The Walkers Stadium, Leicester City.
480. Dave Whelan.

QUIZ NO 49 - GROUNDS (GONE BUT NOT FORGOTTEN)

481. Highbury - Arsenal.
482. Leeds Road - Huddersfield Town.
483. Boothferry Park - Hull City.
484. Maine Road - Manchester City.
485. Ayresome Park - Middlesbrough and Roker Park - Sunderland.
486. The Victoria Ground - Stoke City.
487. The Baseball Ground - Derby County.
488. Burnden Park - Bolton Wanderers.
489. Ninian Park - Cardiff City.
490. The Dell - Southampton.

QUIZ NO 50 - GROUNDS IN GENERAL

491. C - Villa Park.
492. Rugby Park - Kilmarnock.
493. Boundary Park - Oldham Athletic, Deepdale - Preston North End, Kenilworth Road - Luton Town and Loftus Road - QPR.
494. White Hart Lane and Villa Park.
495. Bramall Lane, Goodison Park, Old Trafford and Stamford Bridge.
496. Highbury - Arsenal and Fleetwood Town.
497. St James' Park - Newcastle United and St James Park - Exeter City.
498. Meadow Lane - Notts County and The City Ground - Nottingham Forest.
499. The Den - Millwall.
500. Hampden Park - Glasgow and Queen's Park.

QUIZ NO 51 - HAT-TRICKS

501. Bob Latchford.
502. Alan Shearer and Jimmy Greaves.
503. Peru.
504. Arsenal.
505. Roger Hunt and Fred Pickering.
506. Marco van Basten.
507. Arsenal.
508. Blackburn Rovers and Notts County.
509. They all scored hat-tricks past three different goalkeepers in the same game.
510. West Germany, Poland and Panama.

QUIZ NO 52 - INTERNATIONAL CAPS

511. Dean Saunders.
512. Steven Gerrard.
513. David Platt.
514. Liam Brady.
515. Fulham.
516. Thirty each.
517. Shay Given – 134.
518. Danny Gabbidon.
519. Damien Duff.
520. Billy Wright and Richard Wright.

QUIZ NO 53 - KEEP ON KEEPING ON!

521. Ian Walker for Leicester City.
522. Jack Kelsey.
523. Seaman and Kirkland.
524. John Burridge.
525. Jan Tomaszewski.
526. Arthur Wilkie.
527. Sam Bartram – 1946 and 1947 for Charlton Athletic and Bert Trautmann – 1955 and 1956 for Manchester City.
528. Alex Stepney gives you Stepney Green Tube station, and Mervyn Day produces the rock band Green Day.
529. William 'Fatty' Foulke.
530. Wojciech Szczęsny.

QUIZ NO 54 - LEAGUE CUP 1960-1999 - CLUBS

531. Liverpool.
532. Rotherham United.
533. Middlesbrough.
534. Nottingham Forest.
535. QPR and WBA.
536. Manchester City and Newcastle United.
537. Norwich City.
538. Oxford United and Luton Town.
539. West Ham United.
540. Arsenal and Sheffield Wednesday.

QUIZ NO 55 - LEAGUE CUP 1960-1999 - PLAYERS

541. Gordon Banks.
542. Don Rogers.
543. Terry Venables, John Robertson, Ray Stewart, Nigel Clough and Dean Saunders.
544. Ray Clemence.
545. Steve Morrow.
546. Justin Edinburgh.
547. Les Sealey.
548. Chris Nicholl.
549. Alan Kennedy.
550. Peter Dobing and Jimmy McIlroy.

QUIZ NO 56 - LEAGUE CUP 2000-2022 - CLUBS

551. Birmingham City, Cardiff City and Chelsea.
552. Swansea City and Bradford City.
553. Tranmere Rovers.
554. Aston Villa.
555. Sunderland and Southampton.
556. Arsenal.
557. Spurs and Liverpool.
558. Aston Villa and Birmingham City.
559. Manchester United.
560. Blackburn Rovers, who won, and Bolton Wanderers and Wigan Athletic, who lost.

QUIZ NO 57 – LEAGUE CUP 2000-2022 – PLAYERS

561. Kolo Touré, Emmanuel Adebayor and Mikel John Obi.
562. It referred to Blackburn's Andy Cole, who scored in the Cardiff-based final.
563. Michael Owen.
564. Matt Duke of Bradford City.
565. Ryan Mason.
566. Matt Elliott.
567. Gerrard – Steven and Anthony.
568. Mateja Kežman.
569. Jesse Lingard.
570. Joseph-Désiré Job.

QUIZ NO 58 – FOOTBALL LEAGUE TITLES 1888-1939

571. Preston North End.
572. Sunderland.
573. Aston Villa.
574. Newcastle United.
575. West Bromwich Albion and Burnley.
576. Blackburn Rovers.
577. Everton.
578. Huddersfield Town.
579. Arsenal.
580. Sheffield Wednesday – who were originally known as The Wednesday.

QUIZ NO 59 – FOOTBALL LEAGUE TITLES 1946-1992

581. Stoke City.
582. Portsmouth.
583. Spurs.
584. Manchester United.
585. Chelsea.
586. Aston Villa.
587. Seven.
588. Wolves and Leeds United – the latter's defeat gave Derby the title.
589. Ipswich Town and Nottingham Forest.
590. Wolves.

QUIZ NO 60 – PREMIER LEAGUE TITLES 1992-2022

591. Blackburn Rovers and Leicester City.
592. Manchester City.
593. Arsenal.
594. Manuel Pellegrini – with Manchester City.
595. Chelsea.
596. Norwich City, Newcastle United and Nottingham Forest.
597. 75 points by Manchester United and 100 points by Manchester City.
598. Arsenal – 2003-04.
599. Liverpool – in 2018-19 lost once, with champions Manchester City losing four times.
600. Blackpool, Bournemouth, Bradford City and Brighton & Hove Albion.

QUIZ NO 61 – LINKS

601. They all received 57 England caps.
602. They all advertised Shredded Wheat.

603. They were the first outfielders over 40 to play Premier League football.
604. They were all nibbled at by Luis Suárez.
605. They were top scorers in both the top two divisions of English football.
606. They were all sent off in World Cup finals.
607. They are the only men to score in successive post-Second World War FA Cup finals.
608. They are the only 'Cities' to win the FA Cup.
609. They have all won the FA Cup twice.
610. They are the only four to also win the League title with another club as well.

QUIZ NO 62 - LOCAL DERBIES PART 1

611. It was the only time both League games ended 0-0.
612. WBA and Wolves.
613. B – 7-4.
614. Aston Villa and Birmingham City, with the latter winning.
615. Manuel Pellegrini and David Moyes.
616. 4-4.
617. Sunderland won 9-1 and Newcastle United were champions.
618. Arsenal v Spurs and Sheffield Wednesday v Sheffield United.
619. Crystal Palace v Brighton & Hove Albion.
620. Bristol City v Bristol Rovers.

QUIZ NO 63 - LOCAL DERBIES PART 2

621. Hearts and Hibs.
622. Exeter City and Torquay United.
623. Notts County and Nottingham Forest.
624. Lazio v Roma.
625. Dundee United and Dundee.
626. Norwich City and Ipswich Town.
627. Laurie Brown.
628. It was the only one that took place when the clubs were in different divisions.
629. Port Vale v Stoke City.
630. Burnley and Blackburn Rovers.

QUIZ NO 64 - MANAGERS: BRITISH

631. Herbert Chapman and Brian Clough.
632. Ron Atkinson.
633. East Stirling and St Mirren.
634. Graeme Souness.
635. Don Revie.
636. Bill Nicholson.
637. Harry Redknapp.
638. Howard Wilkinson.
639. Workington, Grimsby Town, Carlisle United and Huddersfield Town.
640. Terry Venables.

QUIZ NO 65 - MANAGERS: FOREIGN

641. Rafael Benítez – with Liverpool.
642. Bob Bradley.
643. Gérard Houllier – with Liverpool.
644. Louis van Gaal, José Mourinho, Ole Gunnar Solskjaer, Ralf Rangnick and Erik ten Hag.

645. Arsène Wenger, Carlo Ancelotti and Pep Guardiola.
646. Gianfranco Zola.
647. Gianluca Vialli, Claudio Ranieri, Luiz Felipe Scolari, Carlo Ancelotti and Maurizio Sarri.
648. Osvaldo Ardiles.
649. Roberto Martínez.
650. Dr Jozef Vengloš.

QUIZ NO 66 – NICKNAMES

651. Newcastle United and Notts County – the Magpies.
652. Forest Green Rovers.
653. Their nicknames can be eaten – Jam Tarts, Toffees, Cherries, Shrimps and Trotters.
654. Oldham Athletic and Wigan Athletic.
655. Tigers v Lions.
656. Terriers v Black Cats.
657. Charlton Athletic, Bristol City and Swindon Town.
658. Their nicknames can be worn – Hatters, Cobblers and Glovers.
659. Brentford and Barnet – the Bees.
660. Crystal Palace – the Eagles would devour Bantams, Seagulls, Bluebirds, Canaries, Owls, Cockerels and Throstles.

QUIZ NO 67 – OCCUPATIONS

661. Mel Nurse.
662. Alan Judge.
663. Peter and Joe Baker.
664. Paul Mariner.
665. Norman Hunter.
666. Steve Cook.
667. Terry Butcher.
668. Brian Miller.
669. Terry Cooper.
670. Tony Waiters.

QUIZ NO 68 – ODD ONE OUT

671. Crystal Palace.
672. Paraguay.
673. Atletico Madrid.
674. Tottenham Hotspur.
675. Bolton Wanderers.
676. Deepdale.
677. Argentina v England – the other three were all decided by penalties.
678. John Aldridge – missed a penalty in an FA Cup final; the others all scored one.
679. Queen's Park.
680. They have all played in an FA Cup final and been relegated in the same season; Wigan Athletic are the odd one out because they won the Cup and all the others lost in the final.

QUIZ NO 69 – ONE-CAP WONDERS PART 1

681. Michael Ball.
682. Ryan Shawcross.
683. Neil Ruddock.
684. Dean Ashton.
685. Joey Barton.
686. Steve Perryman.
687. Colin Harvey.
688. Charlie George.
689. Brian Little.
690. Alan Thompson.

QUIZ NO 70 - ONE-CAP WONDERS PART 2

691. Mark Walters.
692. Bill Foulkes and David Pegg.
693. Gerry Young and Derek Temple.
694. Ken and Tony Brown.
695. John Angus and Gordon Harris.
696. Chris Sutton.
697. Johnny Fantham.
698. Tony Kay.
699. Franny Jeffers and Carl Jenkinson.
700. Phil Boyer and Lee Bowyer.

QUIZ NO 71 - ORIGINS

701. West Ham United v Manchester United.
702. Oldham Athletic v Carlisle United.
703. Everton v Southampton.
704. Watford v Rotherham United.
705. Oxford United v Manchester City.
706. Gillingham v Coventry City.
707. Bristol Rovers v Arsenal.
708. Birmingham City v QPR.
709. Wolves v Tranmere Rovers.
710. Bolton Wanderers v Newcastle United.

QUIZ NO 72 - OUR NAME'S ON THE CUP

711. Lindsay.
712. Wood.
713. Richards.
714. Cook.
715. Norman.
716. Young.
717. Smith.

718. Rush.
719. Johnson.
720. Sanchez.

QUIZ NO 73 - OWN GOALS

721. Bert Turner.
722. Sunderland.
723. Tommy Hutchison and Gary Mabbutt.
724. D - Chris Nicholl.
725. Blackburn Rovers.
726. Jamie Carragher.
727. Paul Robinson.
728. Gary Sprake.
729. Di Napoli scoring against Napoli.
730. Andrés Escobar.

QUIZ NO 74 - PENALTY! PART 1

731. Jan Molby.
732. C - Southend United.
733. 1974 - West Germany v Holland.
734. Andy Johnson.
735. Matt Le Tissier.
736. Gary Lineker v Cameroon.
737. D - John Wark.
738. Diana Ross.
739. Nigel Winterburn.
740. A - George Best.

QUIZ NO 75 - PENALTY! PART 2

741. C - Heath.
742. Glasgow Rangers.
743. Crystal Palace and Brighton & Hove Albion.
744. He scored from the rebound.
745. Four - Oxford United.
746. Francis Lee.

747. Portsmouth.
748. Torquay United.
749. It has never happened.
750. Arsenal and Manchester United – in 2005.

QUIZ NO 76 – PLACES OF INTEREST
751. Dion Dublin.
752. Alan Devonshire.
753. Gareth Barry.
754. Peter Davenport.
755. Alan Cork.
756. Stuart Ripley.
757. Gareth Southgate.
758. Jordan Rhodes.
759. Jimmy Ross.
760. Harry Leyland.

QUIZ NO 77 – PLAY-OFFS
761. Blackburn Rovers.
762. Charlton Athletic and Sunderland.
763. Paul Dickov and Gillingham.
764. Jim Magilton.
765. Sam Allardyce and David Moyes – the clubs were Everton and West Ham United.
766. Scott Sinclair.
767. Bobby Zamora.
768. Kevin Phillips – for Sunderland and Crystal Palace.
769. 5-5.
770. Crystal Palace v West Ham United in 2004 and Fulham v Brentford in 2020.

QUIZ NO 78 – PREMIER PUZZLERS
771. Rob Holding.
772. Peter Crouch.
773. Jordan Pickford.
774. Solly March and David May.
775. Harry Winks.
776. Eden Kane.
777. Nick Pope.
778. Isaac Success.
779. Lewis Dunk.
780. Kyle Walker-Peters.

QUIZ NO 79 – PROMOTION AND RELEGATION PART 1
781. Wolves.
782. Notts County.
783. B – Sheffield Wednesday.
784. Steve Bruce.
785. Oxford United.
786. Crystal Palace and Nottingham Forest.
787. Aston Villa and Blackburn Rovers.
788. Leicester City and Manchester City.
789. Win promotion to Division Two from Division Three South and Division Three North before that geographical organisation of League football was abolished.
790. Preston North End.

QUIZ NO 80 – PROMOTION AND RELEGATION PART 2
791. Newport County – Swansea Town went down with them.
792. Notts County.
793. Reading.
794. Northampton Town and Blackburn Rovers.

795. Arsenal.
796. Swindon Town.
797. West Brom.
798. Wimbledon.
799. Liverpool – in 1893-94.
800. Spurs – in 1919-20.

QUIZ NO 81 – QUOTES PART 1
801. David Platt.
802. Howard Wilkinson.
803. Jack Charlton.
804. Bill Shankly.
805. Jason McAteer.
806. Johan Cruyff.
807. Jasper Carrott.
808. Mick McCarthy.
809. Bob Paisley.
810. Stan Collymore.

QUIZ NO 82 – QUOTES PART 2
811. Jimmy Greaves.
812. Harry Redknapp.
813. Vinnie Jones.
814. Kevin Keegan.
815. John Motson.
816. Ron Atkinson.
817. Alan Brazil.
818. Ryan Giggs.
819. Brian Clough.
820. Roy Keane.

QUIZ NO 83 – REFEREES
821. Anders Frisk.
822. Jack Taylor.
823. Arthur Ellis.
824. Mark Clattenburg.
825. Howard Webb.
826. Dermot Gallagher.
827. Graham Poll.
828. In a 2009 Champions League semi-final he turned down four appeals for a Chelsea penalty and Barcelona's last-minute goal sent them through.
829. He was the only man with one arm to referee an FA Cup final.
830. Clive Thomas.

QUIZ NO 84 – SCOTLAND, WALES, NORTHERN IRELAND AND THE REPUBLIC OF IRELAND IN THE WORLD CUP
831. Uruguay.
832. Northern Ireland and Wales.
833. David O'Leary.
834. Gerry Armstrong.
835. Manager Jock Stein died at the end of the game.
836. Matt Holland scored for the Republic against Cameroon and Holland (the country) failed to qualify.
837. John and Mel Charles.
838. Peter McParland.
839. Archie Gemmill and Trainspotting.
840. Scotland.

QUIZ NO 85 – SCOTTISH FOOTBALL
841. Kilmarnock.
842. It was the only season when neither Celtic nor Rangers were in the top three.
843. Inverness Caledonian Thistle – in 2015.

844. It was the first time that a Scottish club's team contained no Scots.
845. Dundee.
846. Dumbarton and Rangers.
847. St Mirren and Love Street.
848. Aberdeen and Dundee United.
849. Celtic.
850. Dundee United.

QUIZ NO 86 – SENT OFF PART 1
851. Aston Villa.
852. Kevin Moran.
853. Paul Scholes.
854. 12 – Chelsea and Wimbledon.
855. Rob Green.
856. Andrei Kanchelskis.
857. Leeds United.
858. Alan Mullery, Alan Ball and Alan Smith.
859. Chelsea – Victor Moses and Mateo Kovačić.
860. Carlton Palmer.

QUIZ NO 87 – SENT OFF PART 2
861. Pablo Zabaleta and Chris Smalling.
862. Kevin Pressman.
863. Antonio Rattín.
864. QPR and Fulham – Gary O'Neil and Denis Odoi.
865. Roy Keane.
866. Ray Parlour.
867. Terry Hurlock, Mark Walters and Mark Hateley.
868. He was sent off as he came on as a substitute for striking an opponent before play began again.
869. Jan Vertonghen.
870. Mark Dennis.

QUIZ NO 88 – SIX OF THE BEST!
871. B – Huddersfield Town – they lost 7-6 at Charlton Athletic against ten men after leading 5-1.
872. Northampton Town and Luton Town.
873. Sheffield.
874. Scotland in 1881 and Hungary in 1953.
875. Arsenal.
876. England – Liverpool, Nottingham Forest and Aston Villa.
877. Jimmy Armfield, Brian Clough, Jock Stein, Don Revie, Terry Venables and George Graham.
878. Gordon Banks, Peter Shilton, Ray Clemence, David Seaman, David James and Joe Hart.
879. Sunderland.
880. Plymouth Argyle.

QUIZ NO 89 – SUPPORTERS' SONGS
881. Manchester City – Blue Moon.
882. Carousel and Gerry and the Pacemakers.
883. Delilah – Stoke City.
884. McNamara's Band and The Battle Hymn of the Republic, or Glory, Glory Hallelujah.
885. Keep Right On to the End of the Road.
886. Bristol Rovers.
887. Southampton – When the Saints Go Marching In.

888. The Blaydon Races – Newcastle United.
889. West Ham United – I'm Forever Blowing Bubbles.
890. Sussex by the Sea.

QUIZ NO 90 – TEN PLAYERS, PLEASE!

891. Rob Earnshaw.
892. Martin Buchan – Aberdeen and Manchester United.
893. Yakubu.
894. Alex Dawson.
895. Andrei Kanchelskis – for Rangers, Manchester United and Everton.
896. Paul Stewart – for Spurs, Manchester City, Liverpool and Sunderland.
897. Ron Yeats – two League titles and one FA Cup, and Bobby Moore – FA Cup, European Cup Winners' Cup and World Cup.
898. Ron Henry and Thierry Henry.
899. Jay Bothroyd.
900. They have all played for Swindon Town.

QUIZ NO 91 – TRANSFER TRAIL

901. Roma.
902. Marouane Fellaini – he went from Everton to Manchester United while the other three went the other way.
903. Tommy Taylor.
904. Eddie Firmani.
905. Torino.
906. Benfica and PSG.
907. Atletico Madrid, Villareal and Valencia.
908. Nathan Aké – from Chelsea.
909. Lucas Moura.
910. Nathaniel Clyne, Adam Lallana, Rickie Lambert, Dejan Lovren, Sadio Mané and Virgil van Dijk.

QUIZ NO 92 – UEFA CUP 1972-2009

911. Jürgen Klinsmann.
912. Dino and Robert Baggio.
913. Real Madrid and Seville.
914. Inter Milan.
915. The City of Manchester Stadium.
916. IFK Gothenburg.
917. C – Borussia Mönchengladbach.
918. Bobby Robson – with Ipswich Town.
919. Robbie Fowler, Jordi Cruyff and 20.
920. A – Istanbul.

QUIZ NO 93 – WHERE?

921. Brighton & Hove Albion.
922. Burnley.
923. Bournemouth.
924. Swansea City.
925. Tranmere Rovers.
926. Bristol Rovers.
927. Torquay United.
928. Darlington.
929. Port Vale.
930. Nottingham Forest.

QUIZ NO 94 – WORLD CUP 1930-78: COUNTRIES

931. Uruguay and Italy.
932. 1950.
933. 8-3 to Hungary.
934. Hungary and Czechoslovakia.

935. Portugal beat North Korea 5-3.
936. USA and Yugoslavia.
937. Holland.
938. France and West Germany.
939. Argentina.
940. Brazil.

QUIZ NO 95 – WORLD CUP 1930-78: PLAYERS

941. Jairzinho.
942. Daniel Passarella.
943. Just Fontaine.
944. Scoring the goal that beat England for the USA in 1950.
945. Vavá.
946. B – Johan Neeskens.
947. Castro and Ballesteros.
948. 1938 and 1958.
949. Antonio Carbajal – Mexico.
950. Félix and Fillol.

QUIZ NO 96 – WORLD CUP 1982-2022: COUNTRIES

951. Portugal.
952. Belgium.
953. Turkey and South Korea.
954. Sweden.
955. Argentina and Germany (West Germany for the first two).
956. Seven.
957. Uruguay.
958. England.
959. Holland and Croatia.
960. New Zealand – drew all three of their group matches.

QUIZ NO 97 – WORLD CUP 1982-2022: PLAYERS

961. Mbappé (France), Messi (Argentina), Ronaldo (Brazil) and Zidane (France).
962. Mandžukić – Croatia.
963. Brehme (West Germany), Zidane (France), Griezmann (France), Mbappé (France) and Messi (Argentina).
964. Schumacher was the 'keeper and Battiston the forward.
965. Leboeuf, Desailly, Deschamps and Petit.
966. Rossi, Tardelli and Altobelli.
967. Cristiano Ronaldo.
968. Luka Modrić (Croatia).
969. Mauricio Pochettino.
970. Gerd Müller and Thomas Müller.

QUIZ NO 98 – YOU'RE HIRED!

971. Barnsley.
972. Howard Kendall.
973. Ossie Ardiles, Gerry Francis and Christian Gross.
974. West Ham United – David Moyes was the manager.
975. Jean Tigana, Chris Coleman, Lawrie Sanchez, Roy Hodgson and Mark Hughes.
976. Brentford.
977. Stan Cullis, Alf Ramsey, Ron Saunders and Dave Mackay.
978. Ted Drake, Danny Blanchflower, Geoff Hurst, David Webb, Ian Porterfield, Glenn Hoddle, Roberto Di Matteo, Frank Lampard and Ray Wilkins – the

979. They were both goalkeepers in their playing careers and appeared in consecutive FA Cup finals: Fairbrother for Newcastle United in 1951 and Swindin for Arsenal against Newcastle in 1952.
980. Blackburn Rovers, Blackpool, Bolton Wanderers and Preston North End.

QUIZ NO 99 - YOU'RE FIRED!

981. Frank de Boer.
982. Kettering Town.
983. Henning Berg.
984. QPR.
985. Paul Went.
986. Brian Clough and Jock Stein.
987. John Toshack.
988. Bryan Gunn.
989. Alan Ball.
990. Stoke City and Southampton.

QUIZ NO 100 - 'Z'

991. Mário Zagallo.
992. Christian Ziege.
993. Boudewijn Zenden.
994. Zito.
995. Wilfried Zaha.
996. Hakim Ziyech.
997. Dino Zoff.
998. Alexis Sánchez, Mesut Özil, César Azpilicueta, David Luiz, Eden Hazard and the two unused subs: Lucas Pérez and Kurt Zouma.
999. Fazackerley - some sources omit the second 'e' for the Sheffield United man.
1000. Gianfranco Zola.

BONUS - THE QATAR WORLD CUP 2022

1. Ecuador and Uruguay.
2. Saudi Arabia.
3. 15.
4. Julian Álvarez and Olivier Giroud.
5. Ángel Di María and Memphis Depay.
6. Argentina and Croatia.
7. Spain - against Morocco.
8. Belgium.
9. USA.
10. Cody Gakpo.
11. Valencia.
12. Portugal beat Switzerland.
13. Bukayo Saka and Mehdi Taremi.
14. Spain and Costa Rica.
15. Christian Pulisic - Chelsea.
16. True.
17. England.
18. The two Iranian goalkeepers were involved in the first instance of a 'dedicated concussion substitute' in a World Cup match during the game against England.
19. $112 = 64 + 48$.
20. Croatia and Morocco.

BACK PAGE - POLITICAL FOOTBALL

1. Brown
2. David May
3. Eden Hazard and Anthony Eden
4. Baldwin, Wilson and Pitt

Printed in Great Britain
by Amazon